CONVERSATIONS WITH
JORGE LUIS BORGES

CONVERSATIONS
WITH
JORGE LUIS BORGES

RICHARD BURGIN

A CONDOR BOOK

SOUVENIR PRESS
(EDUCATIONAL AND ACADEMIC) LTD

First published in America by Holt, Rinehart & Winston.
First British edition published 1973 by Souvenir Press
(Educational & Academic) Ltd.,
95 Mortimer Street, London W1.

A selection from this book has appeared in *Transatlantic Review
30* under the title "Talking to Richard Burgin." Another
selection from the book has appeared in *Partisan Review*
under the title, "A Conversation with Borges." This selection
appeared in the Winter 1969 issue, Vol. 36, No. 1.

ISBN 0 285 64713 X

*Made and printed in Great Britain by
The Garden City Press Limited,
Letchworth, Hertfordshire SG6 1JS*

CONTENTS

For my Father

PROLOGUE

One of the many pleasures the stars (in which I don't believe) have granted me is in literary and metaphysical dialogue. Since both these designations run the risk of seeming a bit pretentious, I should clarify that dialogue for me is not a form of polemics, of monologue or magisterial dogmatism, but of shared investigation. I can't refer to dialogue without thinking of my father, of Rafael Canssinos-Asseus, of Macedonio Fernandez, and of many others I can't begin to mention— since the most notable names on any list will always turn out to be those omitted. In spite of my impersonal concept of dialogue, my questioners tell me (and my memory confirms) that I tend to become a bit of a missionary and to preach, not without a certain monotony, the virtues of Old English and Old Norse, of Schopenhauer and Berkeley, of Emerson and Frost. The readers of this volume will realize that. It is enough for me to say that if I am rich in anything, it is in perplexities rather than in certainties. A colleague declares from his chair that philosophy is clear and precise understanding; I would define it as that organization of the essential perplexities of man.

I have many pleasant memories of the United States, especially of Texas and New England. In Cambridge, Massachusetts, I spent many hours in leisurely conversation with Richard Burgin. It seemed to me he had no particular axe to grind there was no imposition in his questioning or even a demand for a reply. There was nothing didactic either. There was a sense of timelessness.

7

Rereading these pages, I think I have expressed myself, in fact confessed myself, better than in those I have written in solitude with excess care and vigilance. The exchange of thoughts is a condition necessary for all love, all friendship, and all real dialogue. Two men who can speak together can enrich and broaden themselves indefinitely. What comes forth from me does not surprise me as much as what I receive from the other.

I know there are people in the world who have the curious desire to know me better. For some seventy years, without too much effort, I have been working towards the same end. Walt Whitman has already said it: "I think I know little or nothing of my real life".

Richard Burgin has helped me to know myself.

—Jorge Luis Borges

INTRODUCTION

On the day I found out that Jorge Borges was coming to America, to Cambridge, I ran from Harvard Square to my room in Central Square, over a mile away, in no more than five minutes. The rest of that summer of 1967 seemed only a preparation for his arrival. Everywhere I went I spoke of Borges.

When it was time for school again and I returned to Brandeis for my last year as an undergraduate, I met a very pretty girl from Brazil named Flo Bildner who seemed even more enthusiastic about Borges than I was. Whenever we'd run into each other, we'd talk for three or four hours at a stretch about Borges. After one such conversation, we decided we had to meet him.

I remember the schemes we proposed, elaborate, involuted, outrageous schemes, more complicated than a Russian novel. Finally we rejected all of them. There was only one thing to do; Flo had his telephone number, she should call him up and say we wanted to see him. Strangely, miraculously, the plan worked.

It was November 21, it was grey outside and raining slightly, it was two days before Thanksgiving. Our meeting was set for 6:30 so Flo and I split up in the afternoon, each to go out and buy him a present. Of course, there is something futile about buying a gift for Borges. He simply has no need or desire for any symbol of gratitude for his company. He always makes you feel that it is he who is the grateful one, and that your company is the only gift he needs. In any event,

9

after wandering up and down the long streets of Boston, going through department stores, book stores, and record stores, I finally bought him a record of Bach's Fourth and Fifth Brandenburg concertos on which my father played violin. Back in Cambridge, I met Flo holding her gift, four long-stemmed yellow roses.

The distance from Harvard Square to Borges' apartment on Concord Avenue was only some four or five blocks, yet to us it seemed almost as great an odyssey as the voyage of Ulysses. I think I have forgotton nothing or almost nothing of that evening. I remember the calm in the air after the rain; Flo's eyes as wide and green as tropical limes; the mirrors in the Continental Hotel, where we stopped to perfect our appearance; the thousands of wet leaves on the footpaths. I remember stopping at the wrong address, ringing the doorbell, then apologizing hastily when a young woman answered who had never heard of Borges. I remember how we turned away and ran almost a block laughing—a dreamlike kind of laughter of dizziness, anxiety and an intoxicating kind of happiness.

Then through the glass of a door we saw him, holding a cane and being helped to a lift by a man with crutches. We ran into the building, introduced ourselves, and helped both of them into the lift. The other man, in his early thirties perhaps and a physicist from M.I.T., was helping Borges in his study of Persian literature. Borges was dressed in a conservative but elegant grey suit with a pale blue necktie. The small apartment he shared with his wife seemed peculiarly empty. There were some ten or fifteen books on his bookshelf, a twelve-inch T.V. in the living room and a few magazines on a table. He seemed nervous or ill at ease at first, particularly when we gave him our presents. His wife was out with some friends, so Flo happily assumed the role of woman of the house. She went to the kitchen to fill a vase with water for the roses.

"Don't worry where you sit," he said to me, "I can't see anything." I went to sit down on a couch, but Borges was up again in a start. "Do you want anything to drink? Wine, Scotch, or water?" I declined, but Flo decided to fix everybody a drink. Borges was back in front of me again. "Did you come just to chat or did you have something special to ask me?" If I had known a day or a week before that he would ask this question I wouldn't have known what to say. Now the words came out of their own accord.

"I'm going to write a book about you and I thought I might ask you some questions."

And so we began to talk. Within fifteen minutes we were talking about Faulkner, Whitman, Melville, Kafka, Henry James, Dostoevsky and Schopenhauer. Every five minutes or so he would interrupt the flow of his conversation by saying, "Am I boring you? Am I disappointing you?" Then he said something that moved me very deeply. "I am nearly seventy and I could disguise myself as a young man, but then I would not be myself and you would see through it."

He is, perhaps above all other things, honest—so honest that your first reaction is to doubt him. But as I was to find out, he means everything he says, and when he is joking, somehow he makes sure you know it. Towards the end of our conversation he made some remarks about time. "After two or three chapters of *The Trial* you know he will never be judged, you see through the method. It's the same thing in *The Castle*, which is more or less unreadable. I imitated Kafka once, but next time I hope to imitate a better writer. Sometimes great writers are not recognized. Who knows, there may be a young man or an old man writing now who *is* great. I should say a writer should have another lifetime to see if he's appreciated." Later he would say to me: "... I have uttered the wish that if I am born again I will have no personal memories of my other life. I mean to say, I don't want to go on being Jorge Luis Borges, I want to forget all about him."

That first conversation ended when he said, with the sincerity of a child, "You may win your heart's desire, but in

11

the end you're cheated of it by death." Then he told us he was expected somewhere. He saw Flo and me and the professor to the door and said he hoped I'd call and see him again about the book. He even offered to phone me. "I don't see why it has to end with one meeting," he said.

Three nights later I was back in the same apartment, this time with a tape recorder. Borges began to reminisce about the Argentine poet Lugones. "Lugones was a very fine craftsman, eh? He was the most important literary man of his country. He boasted of being the most faithful husband in South America, then he fell in love with a mistress and his mistress fell in love with his friend." I mentioned that he had dedicated his book *El Hacedor* (translated with the title *Dream Tigers*) to Lugones.

"I think that's the best thing I've done, eh? I mean the idea that I'm speaking to Lugones and then suddenly the reader is made aware that Lugones is dead, that the library is not my library but Lugones' library. And then, after I have created and destroyed that, then I rebuild it again by saying that, after all, I suppose my time will come and then in a sense we'll be contemporaries, no? I think it's quite good, eh? Besides, I think it's good because one feels that it is written with emotion, at least I hope so. I mean you don't think of it as an exercise, no?"

I answered by saying that I understood and admired his idea, but that in my book I wanted a clear picture of Borges and did not want to confuse him with anyone. I added that as he says in "The Aleph," "our minds are porous with forgetfulness," and I was already becoming conscious of falsifying through my memory all that he had said to me. Then I asked him if I could tape record our conversations. "Yes, you can if you want to, only don't make me too conscious of it, eh?"

For the next six months I worked on this book, taping our conversations whenever possible, and as we progressed a pattern began to appear, certain themes and motifs kept recurring. Of course, the book involved more than merely conducting the interviews. I reread Borges, I attended his class on Argentine Literature at Harvard when I could and his series of six Charles Eliot Norton lectures at Sanders Theatre. The lectures were well attended and very well received. Borges had created genuine excitement in the Cambridge intellectual community. I know this meant a great deal to him. "The kind of cheering I got and what I felt behind it is new to me; I've lectured in Europe and South America, but nothing like this has ever happened to me. To have a new experience when you are seventy is quite a thing."

In the middle of December, around the time of her birthday, Flo, who had seen Borges several times on her own, decided to have a dinner party for him and his wife, to be held in my sister's Cambridge apartment. Borges came with his wife and his personal secretary, John Murchison, a Harvard graduate student. Except for the guests of honour, everyone at the party was under twenty-five. This made no difference to Borges, who has always had a marvellous rapport with the young. Later a hippie unexpectedly dropped in on us, but no one, least of all Borges, was upset. "I wonder what the root word of hippie is?" he said. His wife thought the young man's appearance was fascinating. Flo had fixed a delicious, authentic Brazilian dinner, complete with the guitar music of Villa Lobos in the background, and Borges thoroughly enjoyed it. On the way back to his apartment he told me he thought Cambridge was "a very lovable city."

After his successful poetry reading at Harvard (at which Robert Lowell introduced him, saying, "It would be impertinent for me to praise him. For many years I've thought he should have won the Nobel Prize."), I decided that I simply had to arrange a similar affair at Brandeis. With the help of Professor Lida of the Spanish department, who is a friend and devoted admirer of Borges, we set a date for April 1. When I told Borges he said, "Well, I hope it's not all a huge practical joke." Then he asked me if I thought twenty or thirty people might show up. It turned out that over five hundred attended (about a fourth of the school's population) and every seat in one of the university's biggest auditoriums was filled twenty minutes before the programme began.

Downstairs, below the auditorium, Borges was nervously going over what he wanted to say about each poem. This in turn made me nervous, but once he sensed my nervousness, he began joking with me, quite spontaneous jokes really, until we had both calmed down. I had the honour of introducing him, and Mr. Murchison and one of Borges' translators, Norman Thomas di Giovanni, read the poems in translation, after which Borges would comment for two or three minutes about each poem. As I led him onstage, I thought how terrifying it must be for a blind person to face and talk to such a large audience. But once he was onstage, Borges' nervousness vanished. He spoke with a fluency that constantly rose to eloquence. The audience was overwhelmed. When I called him the next day and congratulated him again, he seemed upset and cross with himself. "I always make such a fool of myself."

"But how can you say that?" I said. "Everybody loved it."

"Because I feel it, I feel that I acted like a fool."

By the time of his last lecture at Harvard, Borges was the literary hero of Cambridge. I understand that wherever he went in the country, giving his lectures and poetry readings, his reception was equally enthusiastic. In Cambridge, writers like Robert Lowell, Robert Fitzgerald, Yves Bonnefoy, John Updike and Bernard Malamud attended his lectures and lined up to meet him. John Barth said Borges was the man "who had succeeded Joyce and Kafka."

Borges' response to his long overdue success in America was one of delight and gratefulness, yet he remained, as he will always remain, the most humble and gracious of men. I remember the day I came to see him at the larger and brighter apartment he had just moved into. After ringing his bell, I hesitated in the lobby, a lobby that seemed like a labyrinth to me, with hallways going in every direction and cryptic

14

numbers with arrows underneath them on each wall. But Borges had anticipated my difficulty and with the aid of his cane had walked down three flights of stairs to help me find my way. I was touched, but felt terrible that he had come all the way downstairs on my account. Borges smiled and extended his hand.

BIOGRAPHICAL NOTE

Jorge Luis Borges was born August 24, 1890, in Buenos Aires. At the outbreak of the First World War his family settled in Switzerland, where he finished his secondary education. From 1919-21, he travelled through Spain, was associated with the Ultraist literary group, and published his first poem in the magazine *Grecia*. In 1923, while he was again travelling through Europe, his first book of poetry, *El Fervor de Buenos Aires*, was published in his home country. This was followed by numerous books of poetry, essays, and fiction—among them *Ficciones, Other Inquisitions, Dream Tigers,* and *A Personal Anthology*—as well as a number of works written in collaboration with Adolfo Bioy Casares that included two film scripts. In 1961 he shared, with Samuel Beckett, the $10,000 International Publishers' Prize, and in 1966 the Ingram Merrill Foundation granted him its Annual Literary Award for his "outstanding contribution to literature." Since the 1955 fall of Juan Perón, whom he vigorously opposed, he has been the Director of the National Library of Argentina. During the 1967-68 academic year he was Charles Eliot Norton Professor at Harvard.

R. B.

1

A CHILDHOOD OF BOOKS; BLINDNESS AND TIME;
METAPHYSICS; CERVANTIES; MEMORY;
EARLY WORK; MIRRORS AND APPEARANCES....

BURGIN:
Was there ever a time when you didn't love literature?

BORGES:
No, I always knew. I always thought of myself as a writer,
even before I wrote a book. Let me say that even when I had
written nothing, I knew that I would. I do not think of
myself as a good writer but I knew that my destiny or my
fate was a literary one, no? I never thought of myself as
being anything else.

BURGIN:
You never thought about taking up any career? I mean,
your father was a lawyer.

BORGES:
Yes. But after all, he had tried to be a literary man and
failed. He wrote some very nice sonnets. But he thought that
I should fulfill that destiny, no? And he told me not to
rush into print.

BURGIN:
But you were published when you were pretty young. About
twenty.

BORGES:

Yes, I know, but he said to me, "You don't have to be in a hurry. You write, you go over what you've written, you destroy, you take your time. What's important is that when you publish something you should think of it as being pretty good, or at least as being the best that you can do."

Burgin: When did you begin writing?

BORGES:

I began when I was a little boy. I wrote an English hand-book ten pages long on Greek mythology, in very clumsy English. That was the first thing I ever wrote.

BURGIN: You mean "original mythology" or a translation?

BORGES:

No, no, no, no, no. It was just saying, for example, well, "Hercules attempted twelve labours" or Hercules killed the Nemean Lion."

BURGIN:

So you must have been reading those books when you were very young.

BORGES:

Yes, of course, I'm very fond of mythology. Well, it was nothing, it was just a, it must have been some fifteen pages long . . . with the story of the Golden Fleece and the Labyrinth and Hercules, he was my favourite, and then something about the loves of the gods, and the tale of Troy. That was the first thing I ever wrote. I remember it was written in a very short and crabbed handwriting because I was very shortsighted. That's all I can tell you about it. In fact, I think my mother kept a copy for some time, but as we've travelled all over the world, the copy got lost, which is as it should be, of course, because we thought nothing whatever about it, except for the fact that it was being written by a small boy. And then I read a chapter or two of *Don Quixote*, and then, of course, I tried to write archaic Spanish. And that saved me from trying to do the same thing some fifteen years afterwards, no? Because I had already attempted that game and failed at it.

BURGIN: Do you remember much from your childhood?

BORGES:

You see, I was always very shortsighted, so when I think of my childhood, I think of books and the illustrations in books. I suppose I can remember every illustration in *Huckleberry Finn* and *Life on the Mississippi* and *Roughing It* and so on. And the illustrations in the *Arabian Nights*. And Dickens—Cruikshank and Fisk illustrations. Of course, well, I also have memories of being in the country, of riding horseback in Estancia and Uruguay in the Argentine. I remember my parents and the house with the large patio and so on. But what I chiefly seem to remember are small and minute things. Because those were the ones that I could really see. The illustrations in the encyclopedia and the dictionary, I remember them quite well. *Chambers Encyclopaedia* or the American edition of the *Encyclopaedia Britannica* with the engravings of animals and pyramids.

BURGIN:

So you remember the books of your childhood better than the people.

BORGES: Yes, because I could see them.

BURGIN:

You're not in touch with any people that you knew from your childhood now? Have you had any life-long friends?

21

BORGES:

Well, some school companions from Buenos Aires and then, of course, my mother, she's ninety-one; my sister who's three years, three or four years, younger than I am, she's a painter. And then, most of my relatives—most of them have died.

BURGIN:

Had you read much before you started to write or did your writing and reading develop together?

BORGES:

I've always been a greater reader than a writer. But, of course, I began to lose my eyesight definitely in 1954, and since then I've done my reading by proxy, no? Well, of course, when one cannot read, then one's mind works in a different way. In fact, it might be said that there is a certain benefit in being unable to read, because you think that time flows in a different way. When I had my eyesight, then if I had to spend say a half an hour without doing anything, I would go mad. Because I had to be reading. But now, I can be alone for quite a long time, I don't mind long railroad journeys, I don't mind being alone in a hotel or walking down the street, because, well, I won't say that I am thinking all the time because that would be bragging.

I think I am able to live with a lack of occupation. I don't have to be talking to people or doing things. If somebody had gone out, and I had come here and found the house empty, then I would have been quite content to sit down and let two or three hours pass and go out for a short walk, but I wouldn't feel especially unhappy or lonely. That happens to all people who go blind.

BURGIN:

What are you thinking about during that time—a specific problem or—

BORGES:

I could or I might not be thinking about anything, I'd just be living on, no? Letting time flow or perhaps looking back on memories or walking across a bridge and trying to remember favourite passages, but maybe I wouldn't be doing anything, I'd just be living. I never understand why people say they're bored because they have nothing to do. Because sometimes I have nothing whatever to do, and I don't feel bored. Because I'm not doing things all the time, I'm content.

BURGIN: You've never felt bored in your life?

BORGES:

I don't think so. Of course, when I had to be ten days lying on my back after an operation, I felt anguish but not boredom.

BURGIN:

You're a metaphysical writer and yet so many writers like, for example, Jane Austen or Fitzgerald or Sinclair Lewis seem to have no real metaphysical feeling at all.

BORGES:

When you speak of Fitzgerald, you're thinking of Edward Fitzgerald, no? Or Scott Fitzgerald?

BURGIN: Yes, the latter.

BORGES: Ah, yes.

BURGIN:

I was just naming a writer who came to mind as having essentially no metaphysical feeling.

23

BORGES:

He was always on the surface of things, no? After all, why shouldn't you, no?

BURGIN:

Of course most people live and die without ever, it seems, really thinking about the problems of time or space or infinity.

BORGES:

Well, because they take the universe for granted. They take things for granted. They take themselves for granted. That's true. They never wonder at anything, no? They don't think it's strange that they should be living. I remember the first time I felt that was when my father said to me, "What a queer thing," he said, "that I should be living, as they say, behind my eyes, inside my head, I wonder if that makes sense?" And then, it was the first time I felt that, and then instantly I pounced upon that because I knew what he was saying. But many people can hardly understand that. And they say, "Well, but where else could you live?"

BURGIN:

Do you think there's something in people's minds that blocks out the sense of the miraculous, something maybe inherent in most human beings that doesn't allow them to think about these things? Because, after all, if they spent their time thinking about the miracle of the universe, they wouldn't do the work civilization depends on and nothing, perhaps, would get done.

BORGES: But I think that today too many things get done.

BURGIN: Yes, of course.

BORGES:

Sarmiento wrote that he once met a gaucho and the gaucho said to him, "The countryside is so lovely that I don't want to think about its cause." That's very strange, no? It's a kind of non sequitur, no? Because he should have begun to think about the cause of that beauty. But I suppose he meant that he drank all those things in, and he felt quite happy about them and he had no use for thinking. But generally speaking, I think men are more prone to metaphysical wondering than women. I think that women take the world for granted. Things for granted. And themselves, no? And circumstances for granted. I think circumstances especially.

BURGIN:

They confront each moment as a separate entity without thinking about all the circumstances that lead up to it.

BORGES: No, because they think of . . .

BURGIN: They take things one at a time.

BORGES:

Yes, they take them one at a time, and then they're afraid of cutting a poor figure, or they think of themselves as being actresses, no? The whole world looking at them and, of course, admiring them.

BURGIN:

They do seem to be more self-conscious than men on the whole.

BORGES:

I have known very intelligent women who are quite incapable of philosophy. One of the most intelligent women I know, she's one of my pupils; she studies Old English with me, well, she was wild over so many books and poets; then

25

I told her to read Berkley's dialogues, three dialogues, and she could make nothing of them. And then I gave her a book of William James, some problems of philosophy, and she's a very intelligent woman, but she couldn't get inside the books.

BURGIN: They bored her?

BORGES:
No, she didn't see why people should be poring over things that seemed very simple to her. So I said, "Yes, but are you sure that time is simple, are you sure that space is simple, are you sure that consciousness is simple?" "Yes," she said. "Well, but could you define them?" She said, "No, I don't think I could, but I don't feel puzzled by them." That, I suppose, is generally what a woman would say, no? And she was a very intelligent woman.

BURGIN:
But, of course, there seems to be something in your mind that hasn't blocked out this basic sense of wonder.

BORGES: No.

BURGIN:
In fact, it's at the centre of your work, this astonishment at the universe itself.

BORGES:
That's why I cannot understand such writers as Scott Fitzgerald or Sinclair Lewis. But Sinclair Lewis has more humanity, no? I think besides that he sympathizes with his victims. When you read *Babbitt*, well, perhaps I think in the end, he became one with Babbitt. For as a writer has to write a novel, a very long novel with a single character, the only way to keep the novel and hero alive is to identify with

26

him. Because if you write a long novel with a hero you dislike or a character that you know very little about, then the book falls to pieces. So, I suppose, that's what happened to Cervantes in a way. When he began *Don Quixote* he knew very little about him and then, as he went on, he had to identify himself with Don Quixote, he must have felt that, I mean, that if he got a long distance from his hero and he was always poking fun at him and seeing him as a figure of fun, then the book would fall to pieces. So that, in the end, he *became* Don Quixote. He sympathized with him against the other creatures, well, against the Innkeeper and the Duke, and the Barber and the Parson and so on.

BURGIN:
So you think that remark of your father's heralded the beginning of your own metaphysics?

BORGES: Yes, it did.

BURGIN: How old were you then?

BORGES:
I don't know. I must have been a very young child. Because I remember he said to me, "Now look here; this is something that may amuse you," and then, he was very fond of chess, he was a good chess player, and then he took me to the chessboard, and he explained to me the paradoxes of Zeno, Archilles and the Tortoise, you remember, the arrows, the fact that movement was impossible because there was always a point in between, and so on. And I remember him speaking of these things to me and I was very puzzled by them. And he explained them with the help of a chessboard.

BURGIN: And your father had aspired to be a writer, you said.

BORGES: Yes, he was a professor of psychology and a lawyer.

BURGIN: And a lawyer also.

BORGES:
Well, no, he was a lawyer, but he was also a professor of psychology.

BURGIN: Two separate disciplines.

BORGES:
Well, but he was interested in psychology and he had no use for the law. He told me once that he was quite a good lawyer but that he thought the whole thing was a bag of tricks and that to have studied the Civil Code he may as well have tried to learn the laws of whist or poker, no? I mean they were conventions and he knew how to use them, but he didn't believe in them. I remember my father said to me something about memory, a very saddening thing. He said, "I thought I could recall my childhood when we first came to Buenos Aires, but now I know that I can't." I said, "Why?" He said, "Because I think that memory"—I don't know if this was his own theory, I was so impressed by it that I didn't ask him whether he found it or whether he evolved it—but he said, "I think that if I recall something, for example, if today I look back on this morning, then I get an image of what I saw this morning. But if tonight, I'm thinking back on this morning, then what I'm really recalling is not the first image, but the first image in memory. So that every time I recall something, I'm not recalling it really, I'm recalling the last time I recalled it, I'm recalling my last memory of it. So that really," he said, "I have no memories whatever, I have no images whatever, about my childhood, about my youth. And then he illustrated that, with a pile of coins. He piled one coin on top of the other and said, "Well, now this first coin, the bottom coin, this

28

would be the first image, for example, of the house of my childhood. Now this second would be a memory I had of that house when I went to Buenos Aires. Then the third one another memory and so on. And as in every memory there's a slight distortion, I don't suppose that my memory of today ties in with the first images I had," so that, he said, "I try not to think of things in the past because if I do I'll be thinking back on those memories and not on the actual images themselves." And then that saddened me. To think maybe we have no true memories of youth.

BURGIN: That the past was invented, fictitious.

BORGES:
That it can be distorted by successive repetition. Because if in every repetition you get a slight distortion, then in the end you will be a long way off from the issue. It's a saddening thought. I wonder if it's true, I wonder what other psychologists would have to say about that.

BURGIN:
I'm curious about some of your early books that haven't been translated into English, like the *History of Eternity*? Are you still fond of those books?

BORGES:
No, I think, as I said in the foreword, that I would have written that book in a very different way. Because I think I was very unfair to Plato. Because I thought of the archetypes as being, well, museum pieces, no? But really, they should be thought of as living, as living, of course, in an everlasting life of their own, in a timeless life. I don't know why, but when I first read *The Republic*, when I first read about the types, I felt a kind of fear. When I read, for example, about the Platonic Triangle, that triangle was to me a triangle by itself, no? I mean it didn't have three equal

sides, two equal sides, or three unequal sides. It was a kind of magic triangle made of all those things, and yet not committed to any one of them, no? I felt that the whole world of Plato, the world of eternal beings, was somehow uncanny and frightening. And then what I wrote about the kennings, that was all wrong, because afterwards when I went into Old English, and I made some headway in Old Norse, I saw that my whole theory of them was wrong. And then, in this last book, *A Second Personal Anthology*, I have added a new article saying that the idea of kennings had come from the literary possibilities discovered in compound words. So that virtually there are very few metaphors, but people remember the metaphors because they're striking. They forget that when writers, at least in England, began to use kennings, they thought of them chiefly as rather pompous compound words. And then they found the metaphorical possibilities of those compound words.

BURGIN: What about *The Universal History of Infamy*?

BORGES:
Well, that was a kind of—I was head editor of a very popular magazine.

BURGIN: *Sur*?

BORGES:
Yes. Co-editor. And then I wrote a story, I changed it greatly, about a man who liberated slaves and then sold them in the South. I got that out of Mark Twain's *Life on the Mississippi*, and then I invented circumstances and I made a kind of story of it. But all the stories in that book were kind of jokes or fakes. But now I don't think very much of that book, it amused me when I wrote it, but I can hardly recall who the characters were.

BURGIN:

Would you like *The History of Eternity* to be translated, do you think?

BORGES:

With due apologies to the reader, yes, explaining that when I wrote that I was a young man and that I made many mistakes.

BURGIN: How old were you when you wrote that?

BORGES:

I think I must have been about twenty-nine or thirty, but I matured, if I ever did mature, very, very slowly. But I think I had the luck to begin with the worst mistakes, literary mistakes, a man can make. I began by writing utter rubbish. And then when I found it out I left that kind of rubbish behind. The same thing happened to my friend, Bioy Casares.* He's a very intelligent man, but at first every book he published bewildered his friends, because the books were quite pointless, and very involved at the same time. And he said that he had done his best to be straightforward but that every time a book came out it was a thorn in the flesh, because we didn't know what to say to him about it. And then suddenly he began writing very fine stories. But his first books are so bad that when people come to his house— (he's a rich man)—and conversation is flagging, then he goes to his room and he comes back with one of his old books. Of course, he, well, he hides what the book is, no? And then he says, "Look here, I got this book from an unknown writer two or three days ago, let's see what we can make of it?" And then he reads it, and then people begin to chuckle and they laugh and sometimes he gives the joke away and sometimes he doesn't, but I know that he's reading his own

* Noted Argentinian writer, close friend and collaborator of Borges'.

old stuff and that he thinks of it as a joke. He even encourages people to laugh at it, and when somebody suspects, they will remember, for example, the name of a character and so on, they'll say, "Well, look here, you wrote that," then he says, "Well, really I did, but after all, its rubbish, you shouldn't think that I wrote it, you should enjoy it for the fun of it."

You see what a nice character he is, no? Because I don't think many people would do that kind of thing. I would feel very bashful. I would have to be apologizing all the time, but he enjoys the joke, a joke against himself. But that kind of thing is very rare in Buenos Aires. In Colombia it might be done, but not in Buenos Aires, or in Mexico, eh? Because in Mexico they take themselves in deadly earnest, and in Buenos Aires also. To suggest, for example, that perhaps—you know that we have a national hero called José de San Martín, you may have heard of him, no? The Argentine Academy of History decided that no ill could be spoken of him. I mean he was entitled to a reverence denied to the Buddha or to Dante or to Shakespeare or to Plato or to Spinoza and that was done quite seriously by grown-up men, not by children. And then I remember a Venezuelan writer wrote that San Martín, *"Tenia un aire avieso."* Now *avieso* means sly, but rather the bad side, no? And then Capdevila, a good Argentine writer, refuted him in two or three pages, saying that those two words, *avieso*—sly, cunning, no?—and San Martín, were impossible, because you may as well speak of a square triangle. And then he very gently explained to the other that that kind of thing was impossible. Because to an Argentine mind—he said nothing whatever about a universal mind—the two words were nonsensical. And now, isn't that very strange, he seems to be a lunatic behaving that way.

BURGIN: What about your book *Evaristo Carriego*?

* *

BORGES:

Well, therein a tale hangs. Evaristo Carriego, as you may have read, was a neighbour of ours, and I felt that there was something in the neighbourhood of Palermo—a kind of slum then, I was a boy, I lived in it—I felt that somehow, something might be made out of it. It even had a kind of wistfulness, because there were childhood memories and so on. And then Carriego was the first poet who ever sang the Buenos Aires slums, and he lived on our side of the woods in Palermo. And I remembered him because he used to come to dinner with us every Sunday. I said, "I'll write a book about him." And then my mother very wisely said to me, "After all," she said, "the only reason you have for writing about Carriego is that he was a friend of your father's, and a neighbour and that he died of lung disease in 1921. But why don't you, since you have a year"—because I had won some literary prize or other—"why not write on a really interesting Argentine poet, for example, Lugones."

"No" I said, "I think I can do something better with Carriego," but as I went on writing the book, after I had written my first chapter, a kind of mythology of Palermo, after I had written that first chapter and I had, well, I had begun reading deeply into Carriego, I felt that my mother was right, that after all he was a second-rate poet and I suppose if you get to the end of the book—I suppose a few people have because it's quite a short book—you feel that the writer has lost all interest in the subject and he's doing everything in a very perfunctory kind of way.

BURGIN:

It seems that you began to use your famous image of the labyrinth when you first wrote your handbook on Greek mythology, but I wonder how and when you began to use another of your favourite images, the image of a mirror?

33

BORGES:

Well, that, that also goes with the earliest fears and wonders of my childhood, being afraid of mirrors, being afraid of mahogany, being afraid of being repeated. There are some allusions to mirrors in *Fervor de Buenos Aires*, but the feeling came from my childhood. But, of course, when one begins writing, one hardly knows where to find the essential things. Look here, has this girl gone?

BURGIN: Yes.

BORGES: Well, that's right. She's crazy, this girl.

BURGIN: Why, what happened?

BORGES:

Well, this morning she came, I was in Hiller's Library. Then, all the time she was aiming that machine at me. And I found out that she has had thirty-six shots and then she popped in a moment ago and wanted to have seventeen more.

BURGIN:

What is she doing with them? Is this for herself, or for any magazine?

BORGES:

No, she says that perhaps she'll send them to a magazine. She doesn't know. Thirty-six shots, no?

BURGIN:

You and di Giovanni were working on the translations?

BORGES:

Yes, we were working, yes, but I felt rather, well, I can't be expected to speak or to talk when anyone is around like that.

34

BURGIN:
She was doing them about five inches away from your face?

BORGES: Yes, it was almost a physical assault. Yes, I felt that, I don't know, that somebody had been aiming a revolver at me, no? That she had been aiming a pistol at me, and she kept on at it. Then de Giovanni had the strange idea to tell her to go to Buenos Aires and there she might find other people to photograph and then she got very interested in the idea.

BURGIN:
She wants to make a book of photographs of writers, is that it?

BORGES: Writers, yes.

BURGIN: Of course, a camera is a kind of a mirror.

BORGES: Yes.

BURGIN: A permanent mirror.

BORGES:
Because I'm afraid of mirrors, maybe I'm afraid of cameras.

BURGIN:
You didn't look at yourself much when you could see?

BORGES:
No, I never did. Because I never liked being photographed. I can't understand it.

BURGIN:
Yet your appearance is always very scrupulous. You always dress very well and look very well.

35

BORGES: Do I?

BURGIN:

Yes, of course. I mean you're always very well groomed and attired.

BORGES:

Oh, really? Well, that's because I'm very absent-minded, but I don't think of myself as a dandy or anything like that. I mean I try to be as undistinguished and as invisible as possible. And then, perhaps, the one way to be undistinguished is to dress with a certain care, no? What I mean to say is that when I was a young man I thought that by being careless people wouldn't notice me. But on the contrary. They noticed that I never had my hair cut, that I rarely shaved, no?

BURGIN:

You were always this way, even when you were younger?

BORGES: Always. I never wanted to draw attention to myself.

2

THE LIVING LABYRINTH OF LITERATURE;
SOME MAJOR WORK; NAZIS; DETECTIVE
STORIES; ETHICS, VIOLENCE, AND
THE PROBLEM OF TIME. . . .

BURGIN:

Your writing always, from the first, had its source in other books?

BORGES:

Yes, that's true. Well, because I think of reading a book as no less an experience than travelling or falling in love. I think that reading Berkeley or Shaw or Emerson, those are quite as real experiences to me as seeing London, for example. Of course, I saw London through Dickens and through Chesterton and through Stevenson, no? Many people are apt to think of real life on the one side, that means toothache, headache, travelling and so on, and then you have on the other side, you have imaginary life and fancy and that means the arts. But I don't think that that distinction holds water. I think that everything is a part of life. For example, today I was telling my wife, I have travelled, well, I won't say all over the world, but all over the west, no? And yet I find that I have written poems about out-of-the-way slums of Buenos Aires, I have written poems on rather drab street corners. And I have never written poems on a great subject, I mean on a famous subject. For example, I greatly enjoy New York, but I don't think I would write about New York. Maybe I'll write about some street corner, because after all so many people have done that other kind of thing.

BURGIN:

You wrote a poem about Emerson, though, and Jonathan Edwards and Spinoza.

BORGES:

That's true, yes. But in my country writing about Emerson and Jonathan Edwards is writing perhaps about rather secret characters.

BURGIN: Because they're occult, almost.

BORGES:

Yes, more or less. I wrote a poem about Sarmiento because I had to and because I love him, but really I prefer minor characters or if not, if I write about Spinoza and Emerson or about Shakespeare and Cervantes, they are major characters, but I write about them in a way that makes them like characters out of books, rather than famous men.

BURGIN:

The last time I was here we were talking about your latest book in English, *A Personal Anthology*. Those pieces you decided not to include in it your relegated to a kind of mortality, for yourself anyway. Do you feel you're your own best critic?

BORGES:

No, but I believe that some of my pieces have been overrated. Or, perhaps, I may think that I can let them go their way because people are already fond of them, no? So, I don't have to help them along.

BURGIN:

For example, "The Theologians." You didn't want to include that?

BORGES: Did I include that?

BURGIN: No, you didn't.

BORGES:

Yes, but there the reason was different. The reason was that although I liked the story, I thought that not too many people would like it.

BURGIN: A concession to popular taste.

BORGES:

No, but I thought that since these stories are going to be read by people who may or may not read the other books, I'll try—and besides, people are always saying that I'm priggish and hard and that is something that is very mazy about me—I'll do my best not to discourage them, no? Instead, I'll help them along. But if I offer them a story like "The Theologians," then they'll feel rather baffled, taken aback, and that may scare them away.

BURGIN:

Was that how you felt about "Pierre Menard"—was that why you also excluded it from *A Personal Anthology*?

BORGES:

You know, that was the first story I wrote. But it's not wholly a story . . . it's a kind of essay, and then I think that in that story you get a feeling of tiredness and skepticism, no? Because you think of Menard as coming at the end of a very long literary period, and he comes to the moment when he finds that he doesn't want to encumber the world with any more books. And that, although his fate is to be a literary man, he's not out for fame. He's writing for himself and he decides to do something very, very unobtrusive, he'll rewrite a book that is already there, and very much there, *Don Quixote*. And then, of course, that story has the idea, what I said in my first lecture here, that every time a book is read or reread, then something happens to the book.

BURGIN: It becomes modified.

BORGES:
Yes, modified, and every time you read it, it's really a new experience.

BURGIN:
Since you see the world's literature as constantly changing, as continuously being modified by time, does this make you feel a sense of futility about creating so-called original works of literature?

BORGES: ·
But not only futility. I see it as something living and growing. I think of the world's literature as a kind of forest, I mean it's tangled and it entangles us but it's growing. Well, to come back to my inevitable image of a labyrinth, well it's a living labyrinth, no? A living maze. Perhaps the word labyrinth is more mysterious than the word maze.

BURGIN: Maze is almost too mechanical a word.

BORGES:
Yes, and you feel the "amazement" in the word. With labyrinth you think of Crete and you think of the Greeks. While in maze you may think of Hampton Court, well, not very much of a labyrinth, a kind of toy labyrinth.

40

BURGIN:

What about "Emma Zunz," that's a story of a living labyrinth.

BORGES:

It's very strange, because in a story like "The Immortal" I did my best to be magnificent, while the story "Emma Zunz" is a very drab story, a very grey story, and even the name Emma was chosen because I thought it particularly ugly, but not strikingly ugly, no? And the name Zunz is a very poor name, no? I remember I had a great friend named Emma and she said to me, "But why did you give that awful girl my name?" And then, of course, I couldn't say the truth, but the truth was that when I wrote down the name Emma with the two *m*'s and Zunz with the two *z*'s, I was trying to get an ugly and at the same time a colourless name, and I had quite forgotten that one of my best friends was called Emma. The name seems so meaningless, so insignificant, doesn't it sound that way to you?

BURGIN:

But one still feels compassion for her, I mean, she is a kind of tool of destiny.

BORGES:

Yes, she's a tool of destiny, but I think there's something very mean about revenge, even a just revenge, no? Something futile about it. I dislike revenge. I think that the only possible revenge is forgetfulness, oblivion. That's the only revenge. But, of course, oblivion makes for forgiving, no?

BURGIN:

Well, I know you don't like revenge, and I don't think you lose your temper much either, do you?

BORGES:

I've been angry perhaps, well, I'm almost seventy, I feel

41

I've been angry four or five times in my life, not more than that.

BURGIN:

That's remarkable. You were angry at Perón certainly.

BORGES: Yes. That was different.

BURGIN: Of course.

BORGES:

One day when I was speaking about Coleridge I remember four students walked into my class and told me that a decision had been taken by an assembly for a strike and they asked me to stop my lecturing. And then I was taken aback and suddenly I found that without knowing it I had walked from this side of the room to the other, that I was facing those four young men, telling them that a man may make a decision for himself but not for other people, and that were they crazy enough to think that I would stand that kind of nonsense. And then they stared at me because they were astounded at my taking it in that way. Of course, I realized that I was an elderly man, half blind, and they were four hefty, four husky young men, but I was so angry that I said to them, "Well as there are many ladies here, if you have anything more to say to me, let's go out on the street and have it out."

BURGIN: You said that?

BORGES:

Yes, and then, well, they walked away and then I said, "Well, after this interlude, I think we may go on." And I was rather ashamed of having shouted, and of having felt so angry. That was one of the few times in my life that thing has happened to me.

BURGIN: How long ago was this?

BORGES:
This must have been some five years ago. And then the same sort of thing happened twice again, and I reacted much in the same way, but afterwards I felt very, very much ashamed of it.

BURGIN: This was a strike against the university?

BORGES: Yes.

BURGIN: What were they striking for?

BORGES:
They were striking because there was a strike among the labourers in the port and they thought the students had to join them. But I always think of strikes as a kind of blackmail, no? I wonder what you think about it?

BURGIN: Students are often striking in this country.

BORGES:
In my country also. That they should do it is right, but that they should prevent other people from going to classes, I don't understand. That they should try to bully me? And then I said, well if they knock me down, that doesn't matter, because after all the issue of a fight is of no importance whatever. What is important is that a man should not let himself be bullied, don't you think so? After all, what happens to him is not important because nobody thinks that I'm a prizefighter or that I'm any good at fighting. What is important is that I should not let myself be bullied before my students, because if I do, they won't respect me, and I won't respect myself.

43

BURGIN:

Sometimes values, then, are even more important than one's well-being?

BORGES:

Oh yes, of course. After all, one's well-being is physical. As I don't think physical things are very real—of course they are real, if you fall off a cliff. That's quite real, no? But in that case I felt that whatever happened to me was quite trifling, utterly trifling. Of course, they were trying to bluff me, because I don't think they had any idea of being violent. But that was one of the few times in my life I've been really angry. And then I was very much ashamed of the fact. I felt that, after all, as a professor, as a man of letters, I shouldn't have been angry, I should have tried to reason with them, instead of saying to them "well, come on and have it out," because after all I was behaving in much the same way as they were.

BURGIN: This reminds me a little bit of "The South."

BORGES: Yes.

BURGIN: I think that's one of your most personal stories.

BORGES: Yes, it is.

BURGIN: The idea of bravery means a lot to you, doesn't it?

BORGES:

I think it does because I'm not brave myself. I think if I were really brave it wouldn't mean anything to me. For example, I've been ducking a dentist for a year or so. I'm not personally brave and as my father and my grandfather and my great grandfather were personally brave men, I mean some of them fell in action. . . .

44

BURGIN: You don't think writing is a kind of bravery?

BORGES:

It could be, yes. But perhaps if I were personally brave I wouldn't care so much about bravery. Because, of course, what one cares for is what one hasn't got, no? I mean if a person loves you, you take it for granted, and you may even get tired of her. But if you are jilted, you feel that the bottom is out of the universe, no? But those things are bound to happen. What you really value is what you miss, not what you have.

BURGIN:

You say people should be ashamed of anger, but you don't think people should be ashamed of this; of "what to make of a diminished thing?"

BORGES: I don't think one can help it.

BURGIN: Can you help anger?

BORGES:

Yes, yes, I think that many people encourage anger or think it a very fine thing.

BURGIN: They think it's manly to fight.

BORGES: Yes, and it isn't, eh?

BURGIN: No. It isn't.

BORGES:

I don't think there's anything praiseworthy in anger. It's a kind of weakness. Because, really, I think that you should allow very few people to be able to hurt you unless, of course, they bludgeon you or shoot you. For example, I can't understand anybody being angry because a waiter keeps him waiting too long, or because a porter is uncivil to him, or because somebody behind a counter doesn't take him into account because, after all, those people are like shapes in a dream, no? While the only people who can really hurt you, except in a physical way, by stabbing you or shooting you, are the people you care for. A friend was saying to me, "But you haven't forgiven so and so and yet you have forgiven somebody who has behaved far worse.' I said, "Yes, but so and so was, or I thought he was, a personal friend and so it's rather difficult to forgive him, while the other is an utter stranger so whatever he does, he can't hurt me because he's not that near to me." I mean if you care for people they can hurt you very much, they can hurt you by being indifferent to you, or by slighting you.

BURGIN: You said the highest form of revenge is oblivion.

BORGES:
Oblivion, yes, quite right, but, for example, if I were insulted by a stranger in the street, I don't think I would give the matter a second thought. I would just pretend I hadn't heard him and go on, because, after all, I don't exist for him, so why should he exist for me? Of course, in the case of the students walking into my room, walking into my classroom, they knew me, they knew that I was teaching English Literature, it was quite different. But if they had been strangers, if they had been, well, brawlers in the street, or drunkards, I suppose I would have taken anything from them and forgotten all about it.

BURGIN: You never got into any fights in childhood?

BORGES:
Yes, I did. But that was a code. I had to do it. Well, my

eyesight was bad; it was very weak and I was generally defeated. But it had to be done. Because there was a code and, in fact, when I was a boy, there was even a code of duelling. But I think duelling is a very stupid custom, no? After all, it's quite irrelevant. If you quarrel with me and I quarrel with you, what has our swordsmanship or our marksmanship to do with it? Nothing—unless you have the mystical idea that God will punish the wrong. I don't think anybody has that kind of idea, no? Well, suppose we get back to more . . . because, I don't know why, I seem to be rambling on.

BURGIN:

But this is probably better than anything because it really enables me to know you.

BORGES:

Yes, but it will not be very surprising or very interesting.

BURGIN:

I mean people that write about you all write the same things.

BORGES:

Yes, yes, and they all make things too self-conscious and too intricate at the same time, no? Don't you think so?

BURGIN:

Well, of course it's hard to write about a writer you like; it's hard to write anyway. You wrote a poem roughly about that, didnt' you? "The Other Tiger."

BORGES:

Ah yes, that one is about the futility of art, no? Or rather not of art but of art as conveying reality or life. Because, of course, the poem is supposed to be endless, because the moment I write about the tiger, the tiger isn't the tiger, he becomes a set of words in the poem. "*El otro tigre, el que no esta en el verso.*" I was walking up and down the library, and then I wrote that poem in a day or so. I think it's quite a good poem, no? It's a parable also, and yet the parable is not too obvious, the reader doesn't have to be worried by it, or understand it. And then I think I have three tigers, but the reader should be made to feel that the poem is endless.

BURGIN: You'll always be trying to capture the tiger.

BORGES: Yes, because the tiger will always be . . .

BURGIN: Outside of art.

BORGES:
Outside of art, yes. So it's a kind of hopeless poem, no? The same idea that you get in "A Yellow Rose." In fact, I never thought of it, but when I wrote "The Other Tiger," I was rewriting "A Yellow Rose."

BURGIN:
You often speak of stories as echoing other stories you've written before. Was that the case also with "Deutsches Requiem?"

BORGES:
Ah yes. The idea there was that I had met some Nazis, or rather Argentine Nazis. And then I thought that something might be said for them. That if they really held that code of cruelty, of bravery, then they might be, well, of course, lunatics, but there was something epic about them, no? Now I said, I'll try and imagine a Nazi, not Nazis as they actually are, but I'll try and imagine a man who really thinks that violence and fighting are better than making up things, and peacefulness. I'll do that. And then, I'll make

48

him feel like a Nazi, or the Platonic idea of a Nazi. I wrote that after the Second World War because I thought that, after all, nobody had a word to say for the tragedy of Germany. I mean such an important nation. A nation that had produced Schopenhauer and Brahms and so many poets and so many philosophers, and yet it fell a victim to a very clumsy idea. I thought, well, I will try and imagine a real Nazi, not a Nazi who is fond of self-pity, as they are, but a Nazi who feels that a violent world is a better world than a peaceful world, and who doesn't care for victory, who is mainly concerned for the *fact* of fighting. Then that Nazi wouldn't mind Germany's being defeated because, after all, if they were defeated, then the others were better fighters. The important thing is that violence should *be*. And then I imagined that Nazi, and I wrote the story. Because there were so many people in Buenos Aires who were on the side of Hitler .

BURGIN: How horrible.

BORGES:
It's awful. They were very mean people. But after all, Germany fought splendidly at the beginning of the war. I mean, if you admire Napoleon or if you admire Cromwell, or if you admire any violent manifestation, why not admire Hitler, who did what the others did?

BURGIN: On a much larger scale.

BORGES:
On a much larger scale and in a much shorter time. Because he achieved in a few years what Napoleon failed to do in a longer period. And then I realized that those people who were on the side of Germany, that they never thought of the German victories or the German glory. What they really liked was the idea of the blitzkrieg, of London being on

fire, of the country being destroyed. As to the German fighters, they took no stock in them. Then I thought, well, now Germany has lost, now America has saved us from this nightmare, but since nobody can doubt on which side I stood, I'll see what can be done from a literary point of view in favour of the Nazis. And then I created that ideal Nazi. Of course, no Nazi was ever like that, because they were full of self-pity; when they were on trial no one thought of saying, "Yes, I'm guilty, I ought to be shot; why not, this is as it should be and I would shoot you if I could." Nobody said that. They were all apologizing and crying because there is something very weak and sentimental about the Germans, something I thoroughly disliked about them. I felt it before, but when I went to Germany I was feeling it all the time. I suppose I told you a conversation I had with a German professor, no?

BURGIN: No, you didn't.

BORGES:
Well, I was being shown all over Berlin, one of the ugliest cities in the world, no? Very showy.

BURGIN: I've never been to Germany.

BORGES:
Well, you shouldn't, especially if you love Germany, because once you get there you'll begin to hate it. Then I was being shown over Berlin. Of course, there were any number of vacant lots, large patches of empty ground where houses had stood and they had been bombed very thoroughly by the American airmen, and then, you have some German, no?

BURGIN: No, I'm sorry.

BORGES:

Well, I'll translate. He said to me, "What have you to say about these ruins?" Then I thought, Germany has started this kind of warfare, the Allies did it because they had to, because the Germans began it. So why should I be pitying this country because of what had happened to it, because *they* started the bombing, and in a very cowardly way. I think Göring told his people that they would be destroying England and that they had nothing whatever to fear from the English airmen. That wasn't a noble thing to say, no? In fact, as a politician he should have said, "We are doing our best to destroy England, maybe we'll get hurt in the process, but it's a risk we have to run"—even if he thought it wasn't that way. So when the professor said to me "What have you to say about these ruins?"—well, my German is not too good, but I had to make my answer very curt, so I said, "I've seen London." And then, of course, he dried up, no? He changed the subject because he had wanted me to pity him.

BURGIN: He wanted a quote from Borges.

BORGES: Well, I gave him a quotation, no?

BURGIN: But not the one he wanted.

BORGES:

Not the one he wanted. Then I said, to myself, what a pity that I have English blood, because it would have been better if I had been a straight South American. But, after all, I don't think he knew it.

BURGIN:

He should have read "The Warrior and the Captive" and then he would have found out.

51

BORGES: Yes, he would have found out—yes.

BURGIN:
That's a good story, don't you think? It's very concise.

BORGES: Yes.

BURGIN: You're able to work in . . .

BORGES:
No! I worked in nothing; my grandmother told me the whole thing. Yes, because she was on the frontier and this happened way back in the 1800s.

BURGIN:
But you linked it with something that happened in history.

BORGES: With something told by Croce, yes.

BURGIN: And that's what makes it effective.

BORGES:
Yes. I thought that the two stories, the two characters, might be essentially the same. A barbarian being wooed to Rome, to civilization, and then an English girl turning to witchcraft, to barbarians, to living in the pampas. In fact, it's the same story as "The Theologians," now that I come to think of it. In "The Theologians" you have two enemies and one of them sends the other to the stake. And then they find out somehow they're the same man. But I think "The Warrior and the Captive" is a better story, no?

BURGIN: I wouldn't say so, no.

BORGES: No? Why?

BURGIN:

There's something almost tragic about "The Theologians." It's a very moving story.

BORGES:

Yes, "The Theologians" is more of a tale; the other is merely the quotation, or the telling, of two parables.

BURGIN:

I mean "The Theologians" are pathetic and yet there's something noble about them; their earnestness, their self-importance.

BORGES:

Yes, and it's more of a tale. While in the other I think that the tale is spoiled, by the fact of, well, you think of the writer as thinking himself clever, no? In taking two different instances and bringing them together. But "The Warrior and the Captive" makes for easier reading, while most people have been utterly baffled and bored by "The Theologians."

BURGIN: No, I love that story.

BORGES:

Well, I love it also, but I'm speaking of my friends, or some of my friends. They all thought that the whole thing was quite pointless.

BURGIN:

But I also love "The Garden of Forking Paths," and you don't like that one.

BORGES: I think it's quite good as a detective story, yes.

BURGIN: I think it's more than a detective story, though.

53

BORGES:

Well, it should be. Because, after all, I had Chesterton behind me and Chesterton knew how to make the most of a detective story. Far more than Ellery Queen or Erle Stanley Gardner. Well, *Ellery Queen's* quite a good story.

BURGIN:

You once edited some anthologies of detective stories, didn't you?

BORGES:

I was a director of a series called *The Seventh Circle*, and we published some hundred and fifty detective novels. We began with Nicholas Blake; we went on to Michael Linnis, then to Wilkie Collins, then to Dickens' *Mystery of Edwin Drood*, then to different American and English writers, and it had a huge success, because the idea that a detective story could also be literary was a new idea in the Argentine. Because people thought of them, as they must have thought of Westerns, as merely amusing. I think that those books did a lot of good, because they reminded writers that plots were important. If you read detective novels, and if you take up other novels afterwards, the first thing that strikes you—it's unjust, of course, but it happens—is to think of the other books as being shapeless. While in a detective novel everything is very nicely worked in. In fact, it's so nicely worked in that it becomes mechanical, as Stevenson pointed out.

BURGIN:

I know you've always tried to avoid seeming mechanical in your fiction and also from seeming too spectacular. But I was surprised to hear you say that "The Immortal" was overwritten.

BORGES:

Yes, I think I told you that it was too finely written. I feel that you may read the story and miss the point because of the laboured writing.

BURGIN:

Was the story perhaps inspired by Swift's immortals in *Gulliver's Travels*?

BORGES:

No, because his immortals were very different. They were doddering old things, no? No, I never thought of that. No, I began thinking of the injustice or rather how illogical it was for Christians, let's say, to believe in the immortal soul, and at the same time to believe that what we did during that very brief span of life was important, because even if we lived to be a hundred years old, that's nothing compared to ever-lastingness, to eternity. I thought, well, even if we life to a hundred, anything we do is unimportant if we go on living, and then I also worked in that mathematical idea that if time is endless, all things are bound to happen to all men, and in that case, after some thousand years every one of us would be a saint, a murderer, a traitor, an adulterer, a fool, a wise man.

BURGIN:

The word, or concept, of destiny would have no meaning.

BORGES:

No, it would have no meaning. Consequently, in order to make that idea more impressive I thought of Homer forgetting his Greek, forgetting that he had composed the *Iliad*, admiring a not too faithful translation of it by Pope. And then in the end, as the reader had to be made aware that the teller was Homer, I made him tell a confused story where Homer appears not as himself but as a friend. Because, of course, after all that time he was ignorant. And I gave him

the name of the wandering Jew Cartaphilus. I thought that
helped the tale.

BURGIN:

We seem to be talking about violence and also about the
problem of time, but that's not unusual, really, since you've
often linked these problems, for instance, in a story like
"The Secret Miracle."

BORGES:

Yes, I think I wrote that during the Second World War.
What chiefly interested me—or rather, I was interested
in two things. First, in an unassuming miracle, no? For the
miracle is wrought for one man only. And then in the idea,
this is, I suppose, a religious idea, of a man justifying himself to God by something known only to God, no? God
giving him his chance.

BURGIN: A very personal pact between the two.

BORGES:

Yes. A personal pact between God and the man. And also,
of course, the idea of, well, this is a common idea among
the mystics, the idea of something lasting a very short while
on earth and a long time in heaven, or in a man's mind, no?
I suppose those ideas were behind the tale. Now maybe
there are others. And then, as I had also thought out the idea
of drama in two acts, and in the first act you would have
something very noble and rather pompous, and then in the
second act you would find that the real thing was rather
tawdry, I thought, "Well, I'll never write that play, but I'll
work that idea of the play into a tale of mine." Of course,
I couldn't say that Hladík had thought out a drama or a
work of art and say nothing whatever about it. Because then,
of course, that would fall flat, I had to make it convincing.
So, I wove, I interwove those two ideas. . . . Now that story

has been one of my lucky ones. I'm not especially fond of it, but many people are. And it has even been published in popular magazines in Buenos Aires.

BURGIN:

Maybe they think of it as a more optimistic story of yours, in a way. . . . It ties in with your ideas on time, your "New Refutation of Time."

BORGES:

Yes, yes, and the idea of different times, no? Of different time schemes. Psychological time.

BURGIN:

Another story that I would think of in relation to "The Secret Miracle" is "The Other Death"— I mean in the sense that in both tales the hero tries to extend the properties of time, in one by increasing the amount of experience given to man within a unit of time and in the other by reversing time or a man's life in time.

BORGES:

Ah! That's one of my best stories, I think. But first I thought of it as a kind of trick story. I felt that I had read about a theologian called Damian, or some such name, and that he thought that all things were possible to God except to undo the past, and then Oscar Wilde said that Christianity made that possible because if a man forgave another he *was* undoing the past. I mean, if you have acted wrongly and that act is forgiven you, then the deed is undone. But I thought I had read a story about a past thing being undone.

My first idea was very trivial. I thought of having chessmen inside a box, or pebbles, and of their position being changed by a man thinking about it. Then I thought this is too arid, I don't think anybody could be convinced by it, and then I thought, well, I'll take a cue from Conrad and the idea of *Lord Jim*, Lord Jim who had been a coward and

57

who wanted to be a brave man, but I'll do it in a magic way.

In my story, you have an Argentine gaucho, among Uruguayan gauchos, who's a coward and feels he should redeem himself, and then he goes back to the Argentine, he lives in a lonely way and he becomes a brave man to himself. And in the end he has undone the past. Instead of running away from that earlier battle in one of the civil wars in Uruguay, he undoes the past, and the people who knew him after the battle, after he had been a coward, forget all about his cowardice, and the teller of the story meets a colonel who had fought in that war and remembers him dying as a brave man should. And the colonel also remembers an unreal detail that is worked in on purpose—he remembers that the man got a bullet wound through the chest. Now, of course, if he had been wounded and fallen off his horse, the other wouldn't have seen where he was wounded.

BURGIN:

This feeling of wanting to undo something or to change something in the past also gets into "The Waiting."

BORGES:

Well, that happened. No, because the story, well, of course, I can't remember what the man felt at the end, but the idea of a man who went into hiding and was found out after a long time, this happened. It happened, I think it was a Turk and his enemies were also Turks. But I thought that if I worked in Turks, the reader would feel, after all, that I knew little about them. So I turned him into an Italian, because in Buenos Aires everybody is more or less Italian, or is supposed to know a lot about them. Besides, as there are Italian secret societies, the story was essentially the same. But if I'd given it the real Turkish-Egyptian setting, then the reader would have been rather suspicious of me, no? He would have said, "Here is Borges writing about Turks,

58

and he knows little or nothing about them." But if I write about Italians, I'm talking about my next-door neighbours. Yes, as everybody in Buenos Aires is more or less Italian, it makes me feel I'm not really Argentine because I have no Italian blood. That makes me a bit of a foreigner.

BURGIN:

But what I meant was this idea of regret, which is essentially a metaphysical regret that we feel against an inevitable destiny. I mean, that feeling is in a lot of your stories. For example, "The South" or "The House of Asterion." Speaking of "The House of Asterion," I understand you wrote that in a single day.

BORGES:

Yes. I wrote that in a single day. Because I was editor of a magazine, and there were three blank pages to be filled, there was no time. So I told the illustrator, I want you to work a picture more or less on these lines, and then I wrote the story. I wrote far into the night. And I thought that the whole point lay in the fact of the story being told by, in a sense, the same scheme as "The Form of the Sword," but instead of a man you had a monster telling the story. And also I felt there might be something true in the idea of a monster wanting to be killed, needing to be killed, no? Knowing itself masterless. I mean, he knew all the time there was something awful about him, so he must have felt thankful to the hero who killed him.

Now during the Second World War, I wrote many articles on the war, and in one of them I said that Hitler would be defeated because in his heart of hearts he really wanted defeat. He knew that the whole scheme of Nazism and world empire, all that was preposterous, or perhaps he might have felt that the tragic ending was a better ending than the other, because I don't think that Hitler could have believed in all that stuff about the Germanic race and so on.

59

3

FAVOURITE STORIES; INSOMNIA;
A CHANGING PICTURE; *ALICE IN
WONDERLAND*; *ULYSSES;* ROBERT
BROWNING; HENRY JAMES AND
KAFKA; MELVILLE. . . .

BURGIN:
You seem to disapprove of or criticize so much of your
writing. Which of your stories, say, are you fond of?

BORGES:
"The South" and that new story I told you about, called
"The Intruder." I think that's my best story. And then
"Funes the Memorious" isn't too bad. Yes, I think that's
quite a good story. And perhaps "Death and the Mariner's
Compass" is a good story.

BURGIN: "The Aleph" isn't one of your favourite stories?

BORGES:
"The Aleph," yes, and "The Zahir." "The Zahir" is about
. . . an unforgettable twenty-cent coin. I wonder if you
remember it.

BURGIN: Of course. I remember.

BORGES:
And I wrote that out of the word unforgettable, *"inolvidable";* because I read somewhere, "You should hear so-and-
so act or sing, he or she's unforgettable." And I thought,

well what if there were really something unforgettable. Because I'm interested in words, as you may have noticed. I said, well, let's suppose something really unforgettable, something that you couldn't forget even for a split second. And then, after that, I invented the whole story. But it all came out of the word unforgettable, *"inolvidable."*

BURGIN:

In a sense, that's a kind of variation on "Funes the Memorious" and even "The Immortal."

BORGES:

Yes, but in this case it had to be one thing. And then, of course, that thing had to be something very plain, because if I speak of an unforgettable sphinx or an unforgettable sunset, that's too easy. So I thought, well, I'll take a coin because, I suppose, from the mint you get millions and millions of coins all alike, but let's suppose that one of them is, in some hidden way, unforgettable, and the man sees that coin. He's unable to forget it and then he goes mad. That will give the impression that the man was mad and that was why he thought the coin was unforgettable, no? So the story could be read in two slightly different ways. And then I said, "Well, we have to make the reader believe the story, or at least suspend his disbelief, as Coleridge said. So if something had happened to him before he saw the coin, for example, if a woman he loved had died, that might make it easier for the reader and for myself. Because I can't have the teller of the story buying a package of cigarettes and getting an unforgettable coin. I have to give him some circumstances, to justify what happened to him.

BURGINS: And so you did.

BORGES:

Yes. But those stories go together. "Zahir" is one of the

61

names of God, I think. I got it out of Lang's *Modern Egyptians*, I think, or perhaps out of Burton.

BURGIN:
The story "Funes the Memorious" is, among other things, about insomnia.

BORGES: About insomnia, yes. A kind of metaphor.

BURGIN: I take it, then, you've had insomnia.

BORGES: Oh yes.

BURGIN: I have also.

BORGES: Do you?

BURGIN:
I don't any more, but I have had it. It's a terrible thing, isn't it?

BORGES:
Yes. I think there's something awful about sleeplessness.

BURGIN: Because you think it will never end.

BORGES:
Yes, but one also thinks, or rather one feels, that it's not merely a case of being sleepless, but that somebody's *doing* that to you.

BURGIN: A kind of cosmic paranoia.

BORGES:
Cosmic paranoia, or some fiendish foe, no? You don't feel

it's an accident. You feel that somebody is trying to kill you in a sense, or to hurt you, no?

BURGIN: How long did you have it?

BORGES:

Oh, about a year. In Buenos Aires, of course, it's worse than having it here. Because it goes with the long summer nights, with the mosquitoes, with the fact of tossing about in your bed, having to turn your pillow over and over again. In a cold country I think it's easier, no?

BURGIN: No sleeping pills there?

BORGES:

Oh yes, I had sleeping pills also, but after a time they did me no good. And then there was a clock. It worried me very much. Because without a clock you may doze off, and then you may try to humbug yourself into thinking that you've slept a long time. If you have a clock, then it will give you, the time in the face every quarter of the hour, and then you say, "Well, now it's two o'clock, now it's a quarter past, now half past two, now quarter to three, now the three strokes, and then you go on and on . . . it's awful. Because you know you haven't missed any of the strokes.

BURGIN: What finally got you over the insomnia?

BORGES:

I can hardly remember it, because I had sleeping pills and I also went to another house where there were no clocks, and then I could humbug myself into the belief that I had slept. And finally, I did sleep. But then I saw a doctor, he was very intelligent about it. He told me, "You don't have to worry about sleeplessness because even if you are not sleeping you are resting, because the mere fact of resting, of

63

being in bed, of the darkness, all those things are good for you. So that even if you can't sleep, you don't have to worry." I wonder if it's a true argument, but, on course, that's hardly to the point; the fact is that I did my best to believe in it, and then, once I got over that, that after all a sleepless night meant nothing, I went to sleep quite easily. After a time, of course, as one tends to forget one's painful experiences, I can't tell you what the details were of that period. Is there another tale or poem you want to talk about?

BURGIN:

What about the story "The South"? Now you've said that story is your personal favourite. Do you still feel that way?

BORGES:

But I think I've written a better story called "La Intrusa" and you'll find that story in the last edition of *El Aleph* or of *A Personal Anthology*. I think that's better than the other. I think that's the best story I ever wrote. There's nothing personal about it, it's the story of two hoodlums. The intruder is the woman who comes into the lives of two brothers who are hoodlums. It isn't a trick story. Because if you read it as a trick story, then, of course, you'll find that you know what's going to happen at the end of a page or so, but it isn't meant to be a trick story. On the contrary. What I was trying to do was to tell an inevitable story so that the end shouldn't come as a surprise.

BURGIN:

That's sort of like "The South," though. The sense of inevitability in that story.

BORGES:

Yes, yes. But, I think that "La Intrusa" is better, because it's simpler.

64

BURGIN: When did you write it?

BORGES:

I wrote it about a year or so ago, and I dedicated it to my mother. She thought that the story was a very unpleasant one. She thought it awful. But when it came to the end there was a moment when one of the characters had to say something, then my mother found the words. And if you read the story, there's a fact I would like you to notice. There are three characters and there is only one character who speaks. The others, well, the others say things and we're told about them. But only one of the characters speaks directly, and he's the one who's the leader of the story. I mean, he's behind all the facts of the story. He makes the final decision, he works out the whole thing, and in order to make that plainer, he's the only character whose voice we hear, throughout the story.

BURGIN: Is it a very short story?

BORGES:

Yes, five pages. I think it's the best thing I've done. Because, for example, in "Hombre de la Esquina Rosada," I rather overdid the local colour and I spoiled it. But here I think you find, well, I won't say local colour, but you feel that the whole thing happened in the slums around Buenos Aires, and that the whole thing happened some fifty or sixty years ago. And yet, there's nothing picturesque about it. There are, of course, a few Argentine words, but they are not used because they are picturesque but because they are the exact words, no? I mean if I used any other, I would make the whole thing phoney.

BURGIN:

What about "Death and the Compass"? Do you like the way you treat the local colour in that story?

65

BORGES:

Yes, but in "Death and the Compass," the story is a kind of nightmare, no? It's not a real story. While in "La Intrusa" things are awful, but I think that they are somehow real, and very sad also.

BURGIN:

You've quoted Conrad as saying that the real world is so fantastic that it, in a sense, *is* fantastic, there's no difference.

BORGES:

Ah, that's wonderful, eh? Yes, it's almost an insult to the mysteries of the world to think that we could invent anything or that we needed to invent anything. And the fact that a writer who wrote fantastic stories had no feeling for the complexity of the world. Perhaps in the foreword to a story called "The Shadow Line," a very fine story in Everyman's Library—I think he wrote a foreword to that story—there you'll find the quote. Because, you see, people asked him whether "The Shadow Line" was a fantastic story or a realistic story, and he answered that he did not know the difference. And that he would never try to write a "fantastic" story because that would mean he was insensitive, no?

BURGIN:

I'm curious also about the story "Tlön, Uqbar, Orbis Tertius."

BORGES: One of the best stories I ever wrote, eh?

BURGIN: You didn't include it in your *Personal Anthology.*

BORGES:

No, because a friend of mine told me that many people thought of me as writing cramped and involved tales and she thought that since the real aim of the book was to bring readers nearer to me, it might on the whole be wiser if that story was left out. Because though she liked the story, she thought that it conveyed the wrong idea about me. That it would scare people away from reading the other stories. She said, "For this *Personal Anthology*, you want to make things easier for the reader. While if you give him, well, such a mouthful, you may scare him away and he won't read any of the others." Perhaps the only way to make people read "Tlön, Uqbar, Orbis Tertius" is to make them read other stories first. In Buenos Aires, I mean there are many people who write well, but most of them are trying their hand at realistic stories, no? So this kind of story, of course, falls outside the common expected. That's why I left it out; but it's one of my best stories, perhaps.

BURGIN: You work in your friend Casares again.

BORGES:

Yes, well, yes, that's a kind of stock joke we have of working in imaginary and real people in the same story. For example, if I quote an apocryphal book, then the next book to be quoted is a real one, or perhaps an imaginary one, by a real writer, no? When a man writes he feels rather lonely, and then he has to keep his spirits up, no?

BURGIN:

Of course, it must be much more difficult for you to write now because of your blindness.

BORGES:

It's not difficult, it's impossible. I have to limit myself to short pieces. Yes, because I like to go over what I write, I'm very shaky about what I write. So before I used to write any amount of rough drafts, but now, as I can't do them, I have to imagine drafts. So then, walking up and

67

down the streets or walking up and down the National Library, I think what I want to write, but, of course, they have to be short pieces because otherwise, if I want to see them all at once—that can't be done with long texts. I try to shorten them as much as I can, so I write sonnets, stories maybe one or two pages long. The last thing I wrote, rather a long short story, well, it was six pages.

BURGIN: "La Intrusa."

BORGES:

"La Intrusa," yes. I don't think I'll ever go any farther than that. No, I don't think I'll be able to do it. I want to see at one glance what I've done . . . that's why I don't believe in the novel because I believe a novel is as hazy to the writer as to the reader. I mean a writer writes maybe a chapter, then another, then another one, and in the end he has a kind of bird's eye view of the whole thing, but he may not be very accurate.

BURGIN:

Have you written anything since you've been in America?

BORGES:

I wrote some quite short pieces; I've written two sonnets, not too good ones, and then a poem about a friend who had promised us a picture. He died. He's a well-known Argentine painter, Larco, and then I thought of the picture he had promised us, promised my wife and me—I met him in the street—and then I thought that in a sense he had given us a picture because he had intended to do so, and so the picture was in some mystic way or other with us, except that the picture was perhaps a richer picture because it was a picture that kept growing and changing with time and we could imagine it in many different ways, and then in the end I thanked him for that unceasing, shifting picture, saying that, of course, he wouldn't find any place on the four walls of a room, but still he'd be there with us. That was more or less the plot of the poem. I wrote that in a kind of prose poem.

BURGIN: That's very nice.

BORGES:
Well, I wonder. Now, when I was in New York, I began writing a poem and then I realized it was the same poem I had written to my friend all over again, yes, because it was snowing and we were on the, I don't know, sixteenth floor of one of those New York towers, and then I lay there, it was snowing very hard, we were practically snowed in, snow-bound, because we couldn't walk, and then I felt that somehow the mere fact of being in the heart of New York and of knowing that all those complex and beautiful buildings were around us, that mere fact made us see them and possess them better than if we had been gaping at shop windows or other sights, no? It's the same idea, of course. And suddenly I realized that I'd been going over the same ground, the idea of having something because you don't have it or because you have it in a more abstract way.

BURGIN:
This seems to be the type of feeling one gets from a story like "The Circular Ruins." Can you tell me what the pattern was behind that story?

BORGES:
No. I can't say much about the conception, but I can tell you that when I wrote that story the writing took me a week. I went to my regular business. I went to—I was working at a very small and rather shabby public library in Buenos Aires, in a very grey and featureless street. I had to go there every day and work six hours, and then sometimes

69

I would meet my friends, we would go and see a film, or I would have dinner with somebody, but all the time I felt that life was unreal. What was really near to me was that story I was writing. That's the only time in my life I've had that feeling, so that story must have meant something—to me.

BURGIN:

Have you ever read any poetry by Wallace Stevens?

BORGES:

I seem to recall the name in some anthology. Why? Is there something akin to it?

BURGIN:

I think he believes a lot in the integrity of the dreamer, in the integrity of the life of the imagination as opposed to the physical universe.

BORGES:

Yes, well, but I don't think that feeling got into the story, it was merely a kind of intensity I had. That story came from the sentence "And I left off dreaming about you"—in *Alice in Wonderland*.

BURGIN: You like *Alice in Wonderland*, don't you?

BORGES:

Oh, it's a wonderful book! But when I read it, I don't think I was quite as conscious of its being a nightmare book and I wonder if Lewis Carroll was. Maybe the nightmare touch is stronger because he wasn't aware of it, no? And it came to him from something inner.

I remember as a child I, of course, I greatly enjoyed the book, but I felt that there was—of course, I never put this feeling into words—but I felt something eerie, something

70

uncanny about it. But now when I reread it, I think the nightmare touches are pretty clear. And perhaps, perhaps Lewis Carroll disliked Sir John Tenniel's pictures, well, they're pen-and-ink drawings in the Victorian manner, very solid, and perhaps he thought, or he felt rather, that Sir John Tenniel had missed the nightmare touch and that he would have preferred something simpler.

BURGIN:

I don't know if I believe in pictures with a book. Do you?

BORGES:

Henry James didn't. Henry James didn't because he said that pictures were taken in at a glance and so, of course, as the visual element is stronger, well, a picture makes an impact on you, that is, if you see, for example, a picture of a man, you see him all at once, while if you read an account of him or a description of him, then the description is successive. The illustration is entire, it is, in a certain sense, in eternity, or rather in the present. Then he said what was the use of his describing a person in forty or fifty lines when that description was blotted by the illustration. I think some editor or other proposed to Henry James an illustrated edition and first he wouldn't accept the idea, and then he accepted it on condition that there would be no pictures of scenes, or of characters. For the pictures should be, let's say, around the text, no?—they should never overlap the text. So he felt much the same way as you do, no?

BURGIN:

Would you dislike an edition of your works with illustrations?

BORGES:

No, I wouldn't, because in my books I don't think the visual element is very important. I would like it because I don't think it would do the text any harm, and it might enrich the text. But perhaps Henry James *had* a definite idea of what his characters were like, though one doesn't get that idea. When one reads his books, one doesn't feel that he, that he could have known the people if he met them in the street. Perhaps I think of Henry James as being a finer story-teller than he was a novelist. I think his novels are very burdensome to read, no? Don't you think so? I think Henry James was a great master of situations, in a sense, of his *plot*, but his characters hardly exist outside the story. I think of his characters as being unreal. I think that the characters are made—well, perhaps, in a detective story, for example, the characters are made for the plot, for the sake of the plot, and that all his long analysis is perhaps a kind of fake, or maybe he was deceiving himself.

BURGIN:

What novelists do you think could create characters?

BORGES:

Conrad, and Dickens. Conrad certainly, because in Conrad you feel that everything is real and at the same time very poetical, no? I should put Conrad as a novelist far above Henry James. When I was a young man I thought Dostoevski was the greatest novelist. And then after ten years or so, when I reread him, I felt greatly disappointed. I felt that the characters were unreal and that also the characters were part of a plot. Because in real life, even in a difficult situation, even when you are worrying very much about something, even when you feel anguish or when you feel hatred—well, I've never felt hatred—or love or fury maybe, you also live along other lines, no? I mean, a man is in love, but at the same time he is interested in the cinema, or he is thinking about mathematics or poetry or politics, while in novels, in most novels, the characters are simply living through what's happening to them. No, that might be the

72

case with very simple people, but I don't see, I don't think that happens.

BURGIN:

Do you think a book like *Ulysses*, for example, was, among other things, an attempt to show the full spectrum of thought?

BORGES:

Yes, but I think that *Ulysses* is a failure, really. Well, by the time it's read through, you know thousands and thousands of circumstances about the characters, but you don't know them. And if you think of the characters in Joyce, you don't think of them as you think of the characters in Stevenson or in Dickens, because in the case of a character, let's say in a book by Stevenson, a man may appear, may last a page, but you feel that you know him or that there's more in him to be known, but in the case of *Ulysses* you are told thousands of circumstances about the characters. You know, for example, well, you know that they went twice to the men's room, you know all the books they read, you know their exact positions when they are sitting down or standing up, but you don't really know them. It's as if Joyce had gone over them with a microscope or a magnifying glass.

BURGIN:

I imagine you've revealed a lot about English literature to your students.

BORGES:

Nobody knows a lot about English literature, it's so rich . . . But I believe, for example, that I have revealed Robert Browning to many young men in Buenos Aires who knew nothing whatever about him. Now I'm wondering if Browning, instead of writing poetry—of course he should have written poetry—but I think that many of Browning's pieces would have fared better, at least as far as the reader goes, had they been written as short stories. For example, I think that he wrote some very fine verses in *The Ring and the Book*. We find it burdensome because I suppose we've grown out of the habit of reading long poems in blank verse. But had he written it in prose, had *The Ring and the Book* been written as a novel, and the same story told over and over again by different characters, he might have been more amusing, no? Though he would have lost many fine passages of verse. Then I should think of Robert Browning as the forerunner of all modern literature. But nowadays we don't, because we're put off by the . . .

BURGIN: Poetic technicalities.

BORGES:
Yes, the poetic technicalities, by the blank verse, by the rather artificial style. But had he been, let's say, well, yes, had he been a good prose writer, then I think that we should think of Browning as being the forerunner of what is called modern literature.

BURGIN: Why do you say that?

BORGES:
Because when I told the plots of his poems to my students, they were wild about them. And then, when they read them, they found them, well, a task. But if you tell somebody the framework of *The Ring and the Book*, it's very interesting. The idea of having the same story told by different characters from different angles, that seems to be, well, more or less, what Henry James would have liked to do—a long time before Henry James. I mean that you should think of Browning as having been the forerunner, quite as good as the forerunner, of Henry James or of Kafka. While

today we don't think of him in that way; and nobody seems to be reading him, except out of duty, but I think people should enjoy reading him.

BURGIN:

You've linked Henry James and Kafka before—you seem to associate them in your mind for some reason.

BORGES:

I think that there is a likeness between them. I think that the sense of things being ambiguous, of things being meaningless, of living in a meaningless universe, of things being many-sided and finally unexplained; well, Henry James wrote to his brother that he thought of the world as being a diamond museum, a museum of monsters. I think that he must have felt life in much the same way.

BURGIN:

And yet the characters in James or in Kafka are always striving for something definite. They always have definite goals.

BORGES:

They have definite goals, but they never attain them. I mean, when you've read the first page of *The Trial* you know that he'll never know why he's being judged, why he's being tried, I mean, in the case of Henry James, the same thing happens. The moment you know that the man is after the Aspern papers, you know, well, either that he'll never find the papers, or that if he does find them, they'll be worthless. You may feel that.

BURGIN:

But then it's more a sense of impotence than it is an ambiguity.

BORGES :

Of course, but it's also an ambiguity. For example, "The Turn of the Screw." That's a stock example. One might find others. "The Abasement of the Northmores"—the whole story is told as a tale of revenge. And, in the end, you don't know whether the revenge will work out or not. Because, after all, the letters of the widow's husband, they may be published and nothing may come of them. So that in the end, the whole story is about revenge, and when you reach the last page, you do not know whether the woman will accomplish her purpose or not. A very strange story. . . . I suppose that you prefer Kafka to Henry James?

BURGIN : No, they stand for different things for me.

BORGES : But do they?

BURGIN :

You don't seem to think so. But I think that Henry James believed in society, he never really questioned the social order.

BORGES : I don't think so.

BURGIN :

I think he accepted society. I think that he couldn't conceive of a world without society and he believed in man and, moreover, in certain conventions. He was a student of man's behaviour.

BORGES :

Yes, I know, but he believed in them in a desperate way, because it was the only thing he could grasp.

BURGIN : It was an order, a sense of order.

76

BORGES: But I don't think he felt happy.

BURGIN: But Kafka's imagination is far more metaphorical.

BORGES:
Yes, but I think that you get many things in James that you don't get in Kafka. For example, in Henry James you are made to feel that there *is* a meaning behind experience, perhaps too many meanings. While in Kafka, you know that he knew no more about the castle or about the judges and the trial than you do. Because the castle and the judges are symbols of the universe, and nobody is expected to know anything about the universe. But in the case of Henry James, you think that he might have had his personal theories or you feel that he knows more of what he's talking about. I mean that though his stories may be parables of the subject, still they're not written by him to be parables. I think he was really very interested in the solution, maybe he had two or three solutions and so in a sense I think of Henry James as being far more complex than Kafka, but that may be a weakness. Perhaps the strength of Kafka may lie in his lack of complexity.

BURGIN:
I think of James as being able to create characters; whereas Kafka has no characters, Kafka is closer to poetry really. He works with metaphors and types as opposed to characters.

BORGES: No, there are no characters.

BURGIN: But James could create characters.

BORGES: Are you sure of that?

BURGIN: You don't seem to think so.

BORGES:

No, I think that what is interesting in James are the situations more than the characters. Let's take a very obvious example. If I think of Dickens, I'm thinking of Sir Pickwick, Pip, David Copperfield. I think of people, well, I might go on and on. While if I think of James, I'm thinking about a situation and a plot. I'm not thinking about people, I'm thinking about what happened to them. If I think about *What Maisy Knew*, I think of the framework of a hideous story of adultery being told by a child who cannot understand. I think of that and not of Maisy herself and not of her parents or of her mother's lover and soon.

BURGIN:

You also said that you don't think *Ulysses* has any real characters either.

BORGES: No.

BURGIN:

What do you think of when you think of that book? The language perhaps?

BORGES:

Yes, I think of it as being verbal. I think I said that we know thousands of things about Daedalus or about Bloom, but I don't think we know them. At least I don't. But I think I know quite a lot about the characters in Shakespeare or in Dickens. Now—I'll qualify this, I suppose you can help me out—in the case of *Moby Dick*, I think that I believe in the story rather than in the characters, because the whole story is a symbol, the white whale stands for evil, and Captain Ahab stands, I suppose, for the wrong way of doing battle against evil, but I cannot believe in him personally. Can you?

BURGIN:

To think only in terms of an allegory or a symbol seems reductive of the text, it reduces the story to one of its elements.

BORGES:

Yes, of course it does. That's why Melville said that the book was not an allegory, no?

BURGIN:

But I don't think it's so specific that you can say the whale stands for evil, maybe the whale stands for many things—you feel many things, but you can't perhaps verbalize the exact thing that the whale stands for. I mean I don't like to think of it in terms of algebra, where one thing equals another.

BORGES:

No, no, of course the idea of the whale is richer than the idea of evil.

BURGIN: Yes.

BORGES:

Of course, I'm not allowed to see the work in Melville's mind, but you think of Captain Ahab as being more complex than any abstract statement.

BURGIN:

Yes. Ahab has presence, he has real presence on the page, but I don't really think of him as a real man.

BORGES: I think of Billy Budd as being a real man.

BURGIN: Yes.

BORGES:

And Benito Cereno—but in the case of *Moby Dick*, the whole thing is so overloaded with gorgeous language, no?

BURGIN: Shakespearean, almost.

BORGES:

Shakespearean and Carlylean also, no? Because you feel that Carlyle is in Melville.

BURGIN:

What about "Bartleby the Scrivener"—did you like that story?

BORGES:

Yes, I remember an anthology that came out in Buenos Aires, well, about six months ago. Six Argentine writers could choose the best story they knew. And one of those writers took that story "Bartleby."

BURGIN:

The best story by Melville or the best story by anybody?

BORGES: I mean by anybody.

BURGIN:

One story from all of world literature, that's very difficult.

BORGES:

Yes, but I don't think the aim was really to find out the best stories in the world by any means, I think what they wanted was to get an anthology that people might want us to buy, no? That people might be interested in. Then one took "Bartleby," and one took, I don't know why, a very disagreeable and rather bogus story by Lovecraft. Have you read Lovecraft?

80

BURGIN: No, I haven't.

BORGES:

Well, no reason why you should. And somebody had a story about a mermaid by Hans Andersen, I suppose you know it. Well, it's not a very good story.

BURGIN: Strange choices.

BORGES:

Then somebody had a short Chinese story, quite a good story—three pages long. And then, I wonder what you will make of my choice? I took Hawthorne's "Wakefield," about the man who stays away from home all those years. Well, strangely enough, there were six stories and three by American authors, Melville, Lovecraft and Hawthorne.

BURGIN:

Did you have a hard time picking the Hawthorne from the others or did you know it right away?

BORGES:

No. Well, of course, I really wasn't thinking of all the stories I know. And it had to be a story already translated into Spanish. That limited my choice. Besides, as I didn't want to astonish people, because I think that to take a story by Lovecraft and to say it's the best story in the world, that's done in order to amaze people. Because I don't think that anybody would think that Lovecraft wrote the finest story in the world, if the phrase the finest story in the world can have any meaning. I hesitated between that story and some story by Kipling. And then I thought that that story was a very fine story to be written ever so long ago. The book came out and now there is going to be a second series, by different writers, of course. It was a book that sold very well.

BURGIN:

Have you had occasion to go to Salem since you've been here?

BORGES:

Yes, I went several times to Salem and then I went to Walden also. And I should say that the whole American adventure began here, no? That the history of America began here, in fact, I should say that the West was invented by New Englanders, no?

4

TALES AND MEANINGS; FAVOURITE POEMS;
THE GIFTS OF UNHAPPINESS;
A GIRL FROM BUENOS AIRES;
HOMER; PARABLES. . . .

BORGES:
   You know, I want to tell you that some people have no
literary sense. Consequently they think that if anything
literary pleases them, they have to look for far-fetched
reasons. I mean, for example, instead of saying, "Well, I
like this because this is fine poetry, or because this is a story
that I follow with interest, I'm really forgetting about
myself and I'm thinking of the characters," they're trying
to think that the whole thing is full of half truths, reasons
and symbols. They'll say, "Yes, we enjoyed that tale of
yours, but what did you mean by it?" The answer is, "I
meant nothing whatever, I meant the tale itself. If I could
have said it in plainer words, I would have written it otherwise." But the tale itself should be its own reality, no?
People never accept that. They like to think that writers are
aiming at something, in fact, I think that most people think
—of course they won't say so to themselves or to anybody
else—they think of literature as being a kind of Aesop's
Fables, no? Everything is written to prove something—not
for the sheer pleasure of writing it, or for the sheer interest
a writer may have in the characters or in the situation or in
whatever it may be, no? I think that people are always looking for some kind of lesson, no?

BURGIN:

Maybe they hope that books will give them what the world doesn't. They want some meaning. They want truths. They want to be told how to live, from books.

BORGES:

Perhaps. But if they thought of poetry as they think of music, that might make things easier for them, don't you think so? When you're hearing music, well, of course, I know nothing whatever about music, I suppose you'd just be pleased or displeased or bored. But if you're reading a book, you're hunting for a book behind the book, no? Consequently you have to invent all kinds of reasons. . . . Well, maybe you wanted to ask me something far more concrete, I'm just rambling on. But I think that's the only way for a real conversation to begin by rambling on, no? I'm not looking too closely at what I'm saying.

BURGIN:

No, I think what you say is very true. In the colleges, at least in the schools I've gone to, the method is always to explicate things, explain very literally what everything means.

BORGES:

I'm thinking, for example, that you might have a very crude character in a skit, a comedy or whatever it might be, talking Shakespeare, "Music to hear why hear'st thou music sadly? Sweets with sweets, war not joy delights in joy." Now that's very beautiful, very lovely. And yet you might have a very clumsy and very illiterate character, saying, "If you make music, why do you feel sad. And why does it make you sad?" And it would boil down to the same idea, no? But when Shakespeare says it, it's lovely, and in the other case, I mean if the thought were plainly expressed, it would give you the idea of a very clumsy kind of person, no? Don't you think so?

84

BURGIN: Yes, I do.

BORGES:

I dislike that kind of thing. And another thing I dislike is if people ask me, for example, "Do you admire Shaw?" "Yes." "Do you admire Chesterton?" "Yes." "And if you had to choose between them?" "But I don't." They stand for different moods, don't you think so? I mean you might say that Chesterton as a weaver of tales was cleverer than Shaw, but that on the whole I think of Shaw as a wiser man than Chesterton. But I'm not thinking of a kind of duel between them. Why not have both?

BURGIN:

Things get back to a duel again. Everyone seems to have to prove he's the best.

BORGES:

Well, that's a kind of football mind, no? Or they live a boxing match.

BURGIN: I don't like boxing. Do you?

BORGES:

Yes. At least, when I had sight, I enjoyed seeing a boxing match . . . but as to football, I know so little about it that I could never tell who was who or who was winning or who was losing. The whole thing seemed meaningless to me, and besides, it's so ugly, the spectacle. While a cockfight—you've seen cockfights, no?

BURGIN: No, I haven't. They're banned in America.

BORGES:

Well, they're banned also in my country, but you see them. Besides, a cockfight is a fair fight because both cocks are

85

thoroughly enjoying it, enjoying it, of course, in their own hellish way. I've seen bullfights, also. But to an Argentine, there's something very unfair about a bullfight.

The Spaniards told me that no one thought of danger in a bullfight, because no bullfighters ever run any dangers. They thought of it as sheer technique, and things had to be done in a very elegant way, and that a bullfighter had to be very skilful about it. But that nobody ever thought of a man risking his life, or of a bull being killed, or of the horses being murdered, that those things were not seen. That it was really a game of skill. I said, "Yes, but it's not very skilful to have a bull and some ten or twelve people killing him." Yes," they said, "because you're thinking of the idea of a fair fight, but the idea of a fight isn't there at all. What is really important is that things should be done in a very deft way, it's a kind of dance," And they said, "I see you don't understand anything about bullfighting if you are thinking of it as a dangerous sport or if you're thinking of a man risking his life."

BURGIN:

I think we're constantly trying to block out our distant animal past, and a bullfight is one of the many forms of that idea.

BORGES:

It might be that, but not a very fair form. When my father was a boy, he knew a man, or rather, he knew several men whose job it was to kill jaguars. They were called tigreros because a jaguar is called a tiger, no? Even though it's smaller. The same thing might be found in Venezuela or in Colombia or in southern Brazil. This was in Buenos Aires, I think.

Well, the man's job was to kill jaguars. He had a pack of dogs with him, he had a poncho (a cloak with a hole in it) and a long knife. The dogs would make the jaguar come

86

from his den. Then the man would hold up the poncho in his left hand, moving it up and down. The jaguar would spring, because the jaguar was a kind of machine, it always did the same thing. The jaguar was the same jaguar over and over again, an everlasting jaguar, no? Then he would jump, and as the poncho could hardly defend the man's hands, his hands were scratched by the claws of the jaguar, but at that moment the jaguar laid himself bare to the man's knife and the man killed him with an upward thrust.

I asked my father if the *tigreros* were especially admired and he said no, they did that job even as other men might be cattle drovers or might break in horses or might do any other job, but it was the one thing they did. And they did it skilfully; after all, there were not too many jaguars and sometimes they led a very lazy kind of life. And then men would find out that the sheep or the cattle had been killed by jaguars and they would call the *tigrero*. The *tigrero* would perform that particular job and go on to his own quiet life again. But nobody thought of him as a hero. He was a man who, well, as you might think of a skilful carpenter, or weaver, or sailor. He was a specialized workman.

BURGIN:
And, of course, you wrote a poem about tigers called "The Other Tiger?"

BORGES: Yes.

BURGIN:
Do you think you're more gifted in fiction than in poetry or . . .

BORGES:
I don't think I'm gifted at all. But I don't think of them as different, or different species or tasks. I find that sometimes my thinking or rather my fancy takes the shape of

verse and sometimes the shape of prose, and sometimes it may be a tale or it may be a confession or it may be, well, an opinion. But I don't think they are different. I mean I don't think of them as being in watertight compartments, and I think it's mere chance that a fancy of mine or even an opinion of mine should find its way into prose or into verse. Those things are not essential. You might as well say, you might as well speak about the fact of a book having a grey or a red binding.

BURGES:

In the poem "Matthew 25:30," you say, "And still you have not written the poem." Do you really feel that way?

BORGES:

But that was an actual experience. I felt that an overwhelming number of things had happened to me, and among these things bitterness and misfortune and disappointment and sadness and loneliness and that, after all, those things are the stuff that poetry is made of, and that if I were a real poet, I should think of my unhappiness, of my many forms of unhappiness, as being really gifts. And I felt that I hadn't used them. Of course, in the poem there were good things also, no? For example, Walt Whitman, but most of them, at least as far as I can remember the poem, most of them are really misfortunes. Yet they were all gifts, and the experience was real. When I wrote it, I may have invented the examples I used, but the feeling I had of many things having happened to me and yet of my not having used them for an essential purpose which to me was poetry, that to me was a very real experience. In fact, it made me forget that that afternoon I had been jilted. Of course, those things happen to all men, no? Yes, of course, all men forsake and are forsaken. But when it happens, it's quite important. Well, I suppose it must have happened to you or if not, it will happen in time.

BURGIN: It has.

BORGES:
Well, of course. That's like falling off a horse in my country—everybody does. We're a nation of riders and we all fall off our horses, no?

BURGIN:
In a sense then, all men are more alike than they are different.

BORGES:
Yes, the same idea. But that poem's quite a good one, yes?

BURGIN: Yes.

BORGES:
I think it's quite a fair expression of a true experience, because it really happened to me and it happened in that very place on a railway bridge.

BURGIN:
I also love that poem "The Gifts," which takes place in a library.

BORGES:
That's a very strange thing I found out that I was the third director of the library who was blind. Because first there was the novelist José Mármol, who was a contemporary of Rosas. Then there was Groussac who was blind. But when I wrote that, I didn't know anything about Mármol, and that made it easier. Because I think it was better to have only two, no? And then I thought that perhaps Groussac would have liked it, because I was expressing him also. Of course, Groussac was a very proud man, a very lonely one too. He was a Frenchman who was quite famous in the

Argentine because he once wrote that "Being famous in South America does not make one less well known." I suppose he must have felt that way. And yet, somehow, I hope he feels, somewhere, that I was expressing what he must have felt too. Because it's rather obvious, the irony of having so many books at your beck and call and being unable to read them, no?

BURGIN: Do you have someone read to you now?

BORGES:
Yes, but it's not the same thing. I was very fond of browsing over books, and if you have a reader, well, you can't make them browse. I mean they open the book, they go on reading, if you feel a bit bored you can't tell them to skip a few pages; but rather, you try to receive what they're reading you. And the pleasure of walking to a bookshop, of opening books and looking at them and so on, that is denied. I mean I can only ask, "Have you received any new books in Old English or Old Norse?" And then they say no, and then . . .

BURGIN: You walk out?

BORGES:
Yes, then I walk out. But before I used to spend perhaps a couple of hours every morning, because there were very fine bookshops in Buenos Aires. Now somehow they've died out. Well, the whole city is decaying.

BURGIN: You think so?

BORGES:
Oh yes, we all feel that we are living in a very discouraged, sceptical and hopeless country. Perhaps the only strength our government has lies in the fact that people think that

any other government would be quite as bad, no? That doesn't make for real strength.

BURGIN:

You once wrote these lines, "To have seen nothing or almost nothing except the face of a girl from Buenos Aires, a face that does not want you to remember it."

BORGES:

I wrote that when I was in Colombia. I remember a journalist came to see me, and he asked me several questions about the literary life in Buenos Aires, my own output and so on. Then I said to him, "Look here, could you give me some five minutes of your time?" And he said, he was very polite, and he said "Very willingly." And then I said, "If you could jot down a few lines." And he said, "Oh, of course." And I dictated those lines to him.

BURGIN: They used it as the Epilogue in the *Labyrinths* book.

BORGES: Yes.

BURGIN:

But the reason I mention that to you, well I don't want to over-explicate, but it seems to say that love is the only thing that man can see or know.

BORGES:

Yes, it might mean that, but I think it's not fair to ask that because the way I said it was better, no? But when I was composing that poem, I wasn't thinking in general terms, I was thinking of a very concrete girl, who felt a very concrete indifference. And I felt very unhappy at the time. And, of course, after I wrote it, I felt a kind of relief. Because once you have written something, you work it out of your system, no? I mean, when a writer writes something he's done what he can. He's made something of his experience.

BURGIN:

I've been wondering. I know you like "The Gifts" and "The Other Tiger." Do you have any other favourite poems?

BORGES: The poems I've written or the poems I've read?

BURGIN: No, the poems you've written.

BORGES:

Yes, I think that quite the best poem is the poem called "El Golem." Because "El Golem," well, first, Bioy Casares told me it's the one poem where humour has a part. And then the poem is more or less an account of how the golem was evolved and then there is a kind of parable because one thinks of the golem as being very clumsy, no? And the rabbi is rather ashamed of him. And in the end it is suggested that as the golem is to the magician, to the cabalist, so is a man to God, no? And that perhaps God may be ashamed of mankind as the cabalist was ashamed of the golem. And then I think that in that poem you may also find a parable of the nature of art. Though the rabbi intended something beautiful, or very important, the creation of a man, he only succeeded in creating a very clumsy doll, no? A kind of parody of mankind. And then I like the last verses:

> En la hora de angustia y de luz vaga,
> En su Golem los ojos detenia.
> ?Quien nos dira las cosas que sentia
> Dios, al mirar a su rabino en Praga?*

* At the hour of anguish and vague light,
  He would rest his eyes on his Golem.
  Who can tell us what God felt,
  As He gazed on His rabbi in Prague?

I think that's one of my best poems. And then another poem I like that's quite obvious is "Límites." But I think I can give you the reason. The reason is, I suppose, that it's quite easy to write an original poem, let's say, with original thoughts or surprising thoughts. I mean, if you think, that's what the metaphysical poets did in England, no? But in the case of "Límites," I have had the great luck to write a poem about something that everybody has felt, or may feel. For example, what I am feeling today in Cambridge—I am going tomorrow to New York and won't be back until Wednesday or Tuesday and I feel that I am doing things for the last time.

And yet, I mean that most common feelings, most human feelings, have found their way into poetry and been worked over and over again, as they should have been, for the last thousand years. But here I've been very lucky, because having a long literary past, I mean, having read in many literatures, I seem to have found a subject that is fairly new and yet a subject that is not thought to be extravagant. Because when I say, especially at a certain age, that we are doing things for the last time and may not be aware of it— for all I know I may be looking out of this window for the last time, or there are books that I shall never read, books that I have already read for the last time—I think that I have opened, let's say, the door, to a feeling that all men have. And then, of course, other poets will do far better than I do, but this will be one of the first poems on the subject. So I'm almost as lucky as if I were the first man to write a poem about the joy of spring, or the sadness of the fall or autumn.

BURGIN:
And yet it's the same idea as that parable of yours, "The Witness," where you talk about the infinite number of things that die to the universe with the death of each man.

BORGES: About that Saxon?

BURGIN:
Yes. It's the same kind of idea. Which did you write first?

BORGES:
No, I think I wrote that parable, that story of the Saxon, first.

BURGIN:
So that was really the first time you wrote out the idea.

BORGES:
No, the first time I wrote it I attributed it to a bogus Uruguayan poet, Julio Hacolo—you'll find it at the end of the *Obra Poética*. That was a rough draft.

BURGIN:
Oh, and that preceded the parable and the long poem.

BORGES:
Yes. Somehow I knew that I had found something quite good, but at the same time I didn't think anything could be made of it. So I thought, "I'll jot this down, I can't do anything with it beyond a few lines," and I jotted it down, and some ten or fifteen years after I jotted it down, I came to the conclusion that something more could be done, and then I wrote the poem. Now when I published that very short fragment, nobody remarked on it, because they believed in that bogus book I attributed it to. After all, there was a very good subject, waiting to be picked up by anybody. It was read by most of my friends, I mean by most of the literary men in Buenos Aires and yet they never discovered the literary possibilities. And so I was given ten or fifteen years and then I worked it out in a poem that became quite, well, notorious, let us say, or famous in a sense.

94

So I think those two poems are good. And then there's another poem that I like and that no one seems to have remarked on, except one poet in Buenos Aires. No one seems to have read it, a poem called "Una Rosa y Milton." It's a poem about the last rose that Milton had in his hand and then I think of Milton holding the rose up to his face, smelling the perfume; and of course he wouldn't be able to tell whether the rose was white or red or yellow. I think that's quite a good poem. Another poem about a blind poet. Homer and Milton. And then I think a poem about the sea is quite good, "El Mare."

BURGIN:

You mention Homer, and of course, Homer keeps cropping up in your writing. For example, you wrote a parable about him called "The Maker."

BORGES:

I think that when I wrote that I felt that there was romantic content in the fact of his being aware of his blindness and, at the same time, aware of the fact that his *Iliad* and his *Odyssey* were coming to him, no?

BURGIN:

You often speak of a moment when people find out who they are.

BORGES:

Yes, that's it. Well, that would have been Homer's moment. And then, also, I suppose I must have felt the same thing that I felt when I wrote that poem about Milton. I must have felt the fact that his blindness, in a sense, was a godsend. Because now, of course, that the world had left him, he was free to discover or to invent, both words mean the same thing, his own world, the world of the epic. I suppose those were the two ideas behind my mind, no? First the

95

idea of Homer being aware of his blindness and at the same time thinking of it as a joy, no? And then the idea, also perhaps, that, well, you lose something but at the same time you get something else, and the something else that you get may be the mere sense of loss but at least something is given to you, no? So, maybe, if you're interested in that parable, I suppose you will find behind the parable, or behind the fable, those three feelings.

BURGIN: You really love Homer, don't you?

BORGES:

No, I love *The Odyssey*, but I dislike *The Iliad*. *The Iliad*, after all, the central character is a fool. I mean, you can't admire a man like Achilles, no? A man who is sulking all the time, who is angry because people have been personally unjust to him, and who finally sends the body of the man he's killed to his father. Of course, all those things are natural enough in those tales, but there's nothing noble in *The Iliad*. . . . Well, you may find, I think there may be two noble ideas in *The Iliad*. First, that Achilles is fighting to subdue a city which he'll never enter, and that the Trojans are fighting a hopeless battle because they know that ultimately the city will fall. So there is a kind of nobility, don't you think so. But I wonder if Homer felt it in that way?

BURGIN:

If I might ask you about one more parable, "Parable of the Palace."

BORGES:

Well, the "Parable of the Palace" is really the same parable, the same kind of parable as "The Yellow Rose" or "The Other Tiger." It's a parable about art existing in its own plane but not being given to deal with reality. As far as I can recall it, if the poem is perfect then there's no need for the palace. I mean if art is perfect, then the world is super-fluous. I think that should be the meaning, no? And besides, I think that the poet never can cope with reality. So I think of art and nature, well, nature as the world, as being two different worlds. So I should say that the "Parable of the Palace" is really the same kind of thinking as you get in a very brief way in "The Yellow Rose" or perhaps in "The Other Tiger." In "The Other Tiger" the subject is more the insufficiency of art, but I suppose they all boil down to the same thing, no? I mean you have the real tiger and "*el otro tigre*," you have the real palace, and "*el otro palacia*," they stand for the same thing—for a kind of discord, for the inability of art to cope with the world and, at the same time, the fact that though art cannot repeat nature and may not be a repetition of nature, yet it is justified in its own right.

4—JLB * *

5

FILMSCRIPTS AND FILMS;
THE INVASION; ACTING; LORCA;
PABLO NERUDA; UNAMUNO;
OTHER ARTS. . . .

BURGIN:
I notice that in the book *Discusion* you have some film criticism. You must have been very interested in films at one time.

BORGES: Yes, of course, I was very much interested.

BURGIN: You wrote two filmscripts too, didn't you?

BORGES:
Yes, but they failed. They were published as books, *Los Orilleros* and *El paraíso de los creyente.*

BURGIN: You wrote this in collaboration . . .

BURGIN:
With Bioy Casares. And they would have made very good films. Very good gangster films.

BORGES:
I'd like to see a series of three short films of your stories, of, say, "The Aleph," "The Immortal," "The Garden of Forking Paths," or perhaps "The South." I think "The Aleph" in particular would be a wonderful film.

BORGES:

Of course, it would be. But when someone has decided to make a film of one of my tales, then I have talked to the producer and said, "I think that quite a good film might be made of my story, but don't try to lengthen it."

BURGIN: Better to have a series of two or three.

BORGES:

Yes. And I said, "You better choose two other writers. Take, for example, a story by Cortázar, take a story by Bioy Casares, take one of my stories, then that can be done. But if you take one of my stories and try to stretch it, if you have a long slice of bread and very little butter or if you try to patch it up with local colour, the thing will fail." That's what happened to two of them.

BURGIN: Which two were those?

BORGES:

"Hombre de la Esquina Rosada," and another, I can't recall the name. And they both failed. They both failed because they were full of padding. For example, "Hombre de la Esquina Rosada." They had worked in a horserace, a cock-fight, a tug of war, Negro dances. . . . Now those, they are anachronisms, and besides, even if they were not anachronisms, people feel that such things stop the film. A friend of mine said that if anybody danced or sang in a film he should do it badly. Because otherwise, he said, the film becomes a kind of performance. You might go and see that dance and hear that singing in a theatre or in an opera. So that the only way, if you want dancing or singing, is to have that singing done not too well.

BURGIN: So that it seems more natural?

99

BORGES:

Yes, no, no, because otherwise they stand out as something different. They stop the film. He also said that because beautiful photographs are very easily obtained, he thought Chaplin's idea that beautiful photography isn't necessary was right. Because otherwise the viewer is thinking about the photographers and that's quite as bad as a reader thinking "Here's a purple patch, here's a writer showing off." I think it's an interesting idea. It's an original idea as far as I know. . . . Now I got a letter from a producer in the States saying that he wanted to make a film out of "The Dead Man."

BURGIN: Do you remember his name?

BORGES:

No. I don't. And then I told him that I thought the idea was a very good one but in order that the whole thing shouldn't be grotesque, to us at least, I thought that since there is already a Western tradition, perhaps instead of having a man from Buenos Aires on the Brazilian border, you must have a man from the East in Texas or Arizona, or if not in the real Texas or Arizona, in the Arizona or Texas of Western films, no? Because otherwise I'm afraid that the whole thing would be full of phoney local colour, and they'd have stage gauchos, and they would work in a tango. Of course, the gauchos never heard of tangos in their lives. I said I think it would be wiser if you tried it, if you tried the whole thing, with Western local colour. Of course, Western local colour may be phoney for all I know, but still it's accepted by the imagination. But if you're dealing with sham gauchos and sham compadritos from Buenos Aires, people in Buenos Aires will laugh at it, and people won't care about the film in this country. Or perhaps the local colour will be overflowing the whole story.

100

BURGIN:

What about "The Dead Man"? How do you feel about the story?

BORGES:

"The Dead Man" may be, but I only thought of it after I had written the story, it may be a symbol of all men. Because after all what happens to the dead man is what happens to all of us, I mean, we are given everything, or we are given many things and then they are taken away at one fell swoop. But, of course, I never thought of that. I merely thought of a man thinking he was outwitting a man, feeling that he was in a sense a victor, and at the same time everything he did was unreal. Because they all saw through him. And the chief, the Brazilian, despised him so much that he let him have his horse, his woman, everything, because he knew that the whole thing was unreal and then at the end he had him shot. I think that that's quite a good story, no?

BURGIN:

Yes. It's a very fine story. . . . I wonder how you feel about some of the last movies you saw?

BORGES:

Yes, but now, of course, I can hardly see them, I think that some of the last movies I saw were very good, like *Khartoum*. Did you see it? The story of General Gordon's death?

BURGIN: No. I didn't. What about *Citizen Kane*?

BORGES:

I thought it a very fine film. I saw *Citizen Kane* when it first came out. I didn't like it. I thought it was an imitation of Joseph Von Sternberg. Von Sternberg did it better. Then I saw it again and I said, well, Orson Welles has invented

101

the modern cinema. I think it's a very fine film. But, of course, it's taken from another film called *The Power and the Glory*, you remember, with Spencer Tracy? It's the story of an American businessman who dies and we begin with his funeral, and then his friends begin to talk about him and the story starts within a kind of jigsaw pattern, no? And then, of course, the scheme, the pattern, is more or less the same as *Citizen Kane*, but *Citizen Kane* is a better film. I thought it a very fine film, and the fact, for example, of the palace, of that huge building being so hideous, no? I mean the luxury and the ugliness, and then the essential loneliness of the man, and the fact of his not being a likeable character, because he's not likeable, no?

BURGIN:
No, he's not likeable, but very American, a certain kind of American.

BORGES:
But I wonder if Americans are really like that?

BURGIN: Well, some of them are.

BORGES: Perhaps they are. Most politicians are like that.

BURGIN: They're consumers; they love to accumulate objects.

BORGES:
Well, you think they have the museum feeling or the...

BURGIN: They have a museum complex.

BORGES:
Or rather the idea of grabbing, no? Grabbing, the idea of loot, grabbing, collecting, but of course, I rather like to get away from things.

BURGIN:

Are you fond of Eisenstein's films, *Alexander Nevsky*, for example?

BORGES: No.

BURGIN: I thought you liked epics, though.

BORGES:

I liked that film about the battleship. *Potemkin*. And then I saw it after several years and I thought it quite bad. I thought it was supposed to be a realistic film. I suppose it is. And yet the whole thing is quite unreal.

Let me recall an incident, two incidents, for you. There is a meeting, in Odessa, and then the police, they're supposed to be old hands at that kind of game, have to disperse the crowd. In order to do that, they kill some, I don't know, fifteen or twenty people, and among those people, in order to get pathetic effects, you have a woman with a pram and a child. Then the woman loses her spectacles and the perambulator rolls on a few steps and the child is killed. I remember what Ruskin said about Dickens, "When in doubt, kill a baby." No? Then, after that wholly unreal scene, because I suppose the police knew how to do things without being as clumsy as all that, you have the warship, you have the battleship firing its batteries at the city of Odessa. Now as you don't feel sympathy for the seamen, the only harm the cannons do is to knock a stone lion off its perch. That would be good in a fantastic film, but in a real film I suppose that if there's a battleship within some hundred yards of us and it fires, it should kill somebody, but of course it can't kill anybody or it would ruin the sympathy of the audience, so they merely kill a stone lion. I don't think the Russians are good at realism.

BURGIN: Melodrama?

BORGES:

Melodrama and perhaps a kind of hallucination. But somehow, one never feels anything in a Russian novel to be true because the characters are always explaining themselves to each other.

BURGIN:

What about a writer like Chekhov? Does he appeal more to you?

BORGES:

Chekhov, yes, I think he has a finer touch. But in Dostoevsky, for example, the characters are bound in loud explanations. I don't think people do that kind of thing, but perhaps they do in Russia.

BURGIN:

What about Tolstoy's characters? Are they more alive for you?

BORGES:

I started out reading *War and Peace* and then suddenly I felt that I could not be interested in the characters.

BURGIN: And you didn't read any other books by Tolstoy?

BORGES:

I read some of his short stories . . . I had a sense of effort. And I don't like to have a sense of effort while I'm reading. I mean, if I'm reading a book on mathematics, or psychology, or science, then that's as it should be, but in a novel or a tale, I don't want to have a sense of effort. I want to enjoy myself. I don't see why a writer of stories or of novels should give any trouble. I remember George Moore wrote about Tolstoy that he described twelve jury men in such a minute way that when you got to the fourth one, you had forgotten all about the first one. And then he said that Tolstoy perhaps woke up at night when he was writing a novel and said, "Well I haven't worked in a horserace, there's no description of a ball, there should be people playing at cards." That's unfair, of course. But if I had to choose between English and Russian literature or let's say between Dickens and Dostoevsky, I would choose Dickens. Because I think of Dickens as being truer to life, perhaps larger than life. And I think Dickens is underrated now, though Chesterton did what he could for him.

BURGIN:

I know you're working on a screen play now. Since you can't see so well, I wonder how you can go about it? It must confront you with difficulties.

BORGES:

Well, no, but I've written only the dialogue. Besides, I can imagine, I've seen hundreds or thousands of films in my time, I can imagine a film.

BURGIN:

I know that you've, of course, written some film criticism.

BORGES:

Oh yes. I'm very fond of films. In Buenos Aires people go to films far more than they do here. In Buenos Aires, every day, well I suppose you can choose between forty different films, and those films, well, most of them are American, but you can also have your pick of Swedish, English, French, Italian or even Russian films.

BURGIN:

Why don't you tell me something about the plot of your movie, *The Invasion*?

105

BORGES:

Well, the plot is, the central plot should be that a city is about to be invaded and then—the whole thing is rather fantastic—the authorities take no measures whatsoever. The invaders are very ruthless and very powerful and then the city is defended.

BURGIN: The invaders, who are they?

BORGES:

Well, you don't know. The invaders, you see them and you feel that they are very ruthless and very efficient and many. And, of course, you have a conflict. All this has no political meaning—we were not thinking, say, of the communists, or the fascists, and then the city is defended by an old gentleman and his friends. Now his friends are very half-hearted, they are very sceptical about the whole thing and they are bound by circumstance. For example, a man has to go and save his country, but he can't do that because he has to go with his wife to a party or because he had a bad cold, no? And, yet somehow those people in their half-hearted sceptical, unbelieving way defend the city. And then, in the end, the city falls out of the hands of the enemies and you know that the defenders will go on fighting, somehow. That's the story, not a very impressive story as I tell you, but it makes quite a good film. And then, you see those people are rather helpless, some of them are even figures of fun, and yet somehow they get away with it and they defend the city successfully. And, of course, the whole thing has many adventures, because you have these people rushing to and fro.

BURGIN: There seems to be an epic quality about the film.

BORGES:

An epic quality, yes, and at the same time, the whole thing

106

is rather desultory. Those people may, when they are in a great hurry, they may have a poker game or a card game and they'll be losing time over that, or a man may have an assignation with a girl and may forget all about the invaders. I think it's quite a good film. Of course, as I tell it to you, it doesn't sound like a good film, but . . .

I think it should be a very amusing film also, because you have all those kinds of characters, the characters are quite unlike each other and there are, well, for example, there *are* some epic moments. There is a man who's a coward and he is one of the defenders. And the others, they accept him, they're all friends. And they say, "Yes, so and so, well he isn't too good, no? I don't think we can count on him, no?" Because they know that he's a coward. And then, there is a moment when one of them has to get himself killed. Well, they have to send somebody, and this man who is a coward says, "Look here, I want to go. Yes," he says, "after all you are very efficient men, you are brave men, you *can* be helpful. What can I do? You have been very kind to me, all of you, but I know the way you feel about me and besides, what is more important, I know the way I feel about myself. The only thing I can do is to die. So let me go." And then the other says "Thank you" and he shakes hands with him. And another is just about to shake hands with him, but he thinks better of it because he feels that if he shakes hands, he is acknowledging that the other is right that he will die, and then the man does go off and gets killed. And there are many moments of that kind, no?

BURGIN: Yes, I see.

BORGES:
Yes, but that's a good moment, no? When a man says "The only thing I can do is to die. After all, I'm not very good at fighting but I have one advantage, I can get myself killed as well as anybody precisely because I *am* a coward." And

107

one of them pats him on the back and they all feel very uncomfortable and then they say, "Oh no, you'll do fine, we wish you luck." And he goes off grinning and they know he's going to die.

There are many episodes of that kind. And there's a love interest also. There is a man—he's in love—and he doesn't want his lady to know that he is risking his life. So he invents all sorts of excuses. Sometimes she takes him to task, and says, "I feel you are really more in love with those schemes than with me." But he says, "No, you know that I love you," and they make plans. But in the end, it comes out that she knows all about it. But that she doesn't want him to be worried thinking she knows.

I think it's quite a good film. I'm telling you those two episodes, they're the ones that come to mind, but there are more. And, of course, as I was saying to Santiago, it's quite unlike any other Argentine film.

BURGIN:
Do you know anything about this director? Is he a prominent director in your country?

BORGES:
No. He's been working in Europe, but in quite a minor capacity for seven or eight years and he's a personal friend of a very famous English director. I can't recall the name. He knows a lot of the technical side. And he evolved the plan. And the central character is based upon a friend of mine named Fernandez, a humorist, but a metaphysical humorist. I think it should be quite a good film, but if they muff it, well, you never can tell, no? Now I'm rather worried because Santiago says that he's found the most wonderful actress on earth and that he's also about to be married. But I'm afraid that he's about to be married to the most wonderful actress, and the most wonderful actress may be no good as far as I know.

BURGIN: He's going to marry the main actress in the film?

BORGES:
Yes, that's what I'm afraid of, because he says, "I've discovered the most wonderful actress in Paris." I don't like that because why should he discover in Paris a wonderful actress for a film to be acted in Buenos Aires? Of course, she may be Argentine for all I know, and then he says, "Also, I want you to know that I'm going to be married." But I'm afraid that both ladies may be the same and in that case we'll have to put up with somebody merely because he's in love with her and she's his wife. That doesn't do us any good, no? But of course, if he found a fine actress, and he's married to another lady, then that's all right, no?

BURGIN: Have you ever been interested in acting?

BORGES:
No. . . . Now I wonder if I told you, when I read O'Neill, I was hardly impressed by him. And then I went to see *The Great God Brown* and I was overwhelmed. Because when you don't *see* the masks they make no impression whatever on you, no? "So and so puts on a mask, they take the mask, the mask is left on the table." You think of all that as being rather silly. And rather childish. But when you see it *acted*, it is quite different.

But maybe I'm being unfair to O'Neill. It could be because I've read Bernard Shaw, and Shaw wrote his plays, published his plays, in order that they could be read as novels. In Shaw's plays you get long descriptions of furniture, even of the bookshelves, you get long descriptions of the characters, you can imagine them. But in the case of O'Neill he says, "A comes in, B comes in." You don't know what to expect them to look like or what they are, no? No, he didn't make his plays for reading but to be acted.

109

BURGIN: What about the plays of Lorca?

BORGES: I don't like them. I never could enjoy Lorca.

BURGIN: Or his poetry either?

BORGES:
No. I saw *Yerma* and I found it so silly that I walked away.
I couldn't stand it. Yet I suppose that's a blind spot
because . . .

BURGIN: Lorca, for some reason, is idealized in this country.

BORGES:
I suppose he had the good luck to be executed, no? I had
an hour's chat with him in Buenos Aires. He struck me as
a kind of play actor, no? Living up to a certain role. I mean
being a professional Andalusian.

BURGIN:
The way Cocteau was supposed to be, as I understand it.

BORGES:
Yes, I suppose he was. But in the case of Lorca, it was very
strange because I lived in Andalusia and the Andalusians
aren't a bit like that. His were stage Andalusians. Maybe he
thought that in Buenos Aires he had to live up to that
character, but in Andalusia, people are not like that. In fact,
if you are in Andalusia, if you are talking to a man of letters
and you speak to him about bullfights, he'll say, "Oh well,
that sort of thing pleases people, I suppose, but really the
torero works in no danger whatever." Because they are
bored by those things, because every writer is bored by
the local colour in his own country, no? Well, when I met
Lorca he was being a professional Andalusian.

110

BURGIN:

You met Lorca only one time? You never met again?

BORGES: No.

BURGIN:

And Sartre you also met one time and then never again?

BORGES:

No, but Sartre is a more intelligent man than Lorca. Besides, Lorca wanted to astonish us. He said to me that he was very much troubled about a very important character in the contemporary world. A character in whom you could see all the tragedy of American life. And then he went on in this way until I asked him who was this character and it turned out the character was *Mickey Mouse*. I suppose he was trying to be clever. And I thought, that's the kind of thing you might say when you are very very young and you want to astonish somebody. But after all, he was a grown man, he had no need, he could have talked in a different way. But when he started in about Mickey Mouse being a symbol of America, there was a friend of mine there and he looked at me and I looked at him and we both walked away because we were both too old for that kind of game, no? Even at the time.

BURGIN: When was that?

BORGES:

Oh, years and years ago. Even then we felt that that was what you call sophomoric.

BURGIN:

Well, Lorca wasn't a thinker, but I think he had a gift for words.

111

BORGES: But I think there is very little behind the words.

BURGIN: He had a gift for hearing words.

BORGES:
Well, a gift for gab. For example, he makes striking meta-phors, but I wonder if he makes striking metaphors for *him*, because I think that his world was mostly verbal. I think that he was fond of playing words against each other, the contrast of words, but I wonder if he knew what he was doing.

BURGIN:
What about Pablo Neruda? You've met him, haven't you?

BORGES:
I met him once. And we were both quite young at the time. And then we fell to speaking of the Spanish language. And we came to the conclusion that nothing could be done with it, because it was such a clumsy language, and I said that was the reason that nothing whatever had ever been done with it and he said, "Well, of course, there's no Spanish literature, no?" and I said, "Well, of course not." And then we went on in that way. The whole thing was a kind of joke.

BURGIN: I know you admire his poetry, don't you?

BORGES:
I think of him as a very fine poet, a very fine poet. I don't admire him as a man, I think of him as a very mean man.

BURGIN: Why do you say that?

BORGES:
Well, he wrote a book—well, maybe here I'm being political —he wrote a book about the tyrants of South America, and then he had several stanzas against the United States. Now

he knows that that's rubbish. And he had not a word against Perón. Because he had a law suit in Buenos Aires, that was explained to me afterwards, and he didn't care to risk anything. And so, when he was supposed to be writing at the top of his voice, full of noble indignation, he had not a word to say against Perón. And he was married to an Argentine lady, he knew that many of his friends had been sent to jail. He knew all about the state of our country, but not a word against him. At the same time he was speaking against the United States, knowing that the whole thing was a lie, no? But, of course, that doesn't mean anything against his poetry. Neruda is a very fine poet, a great poet in fact. And when that man got the Nobel Prize,* I said that it should have been given to Neruda!

Now when I was in Chile, and we were on different political sides, I think he did quite the best thing to do. He went on a holiday during that three or four days I was there so there was no occasion for our meeting. But I think that he was acting politely, no? Because he knew that people would be playing him up against me, no? I mean I was an Argentine poet, he a Chilean poet, he's on the side of the Communists, I'm against them. So I felt that he was behaving very wisely in avoiding a meeting that would be quite uncomfortable for both of us.

BURGIN: Now Unamuno you never met.

BORGES: But he sent me a very nice letter.

BURGIN:
Yes, I think you mentioned it. It was about infinity.

BORGES:
Yes. Unamuno's a very great writer. I admire Unamuno greatly.

* Miguel de Asturias, winner of the 1968 Nobel Prize for Literature.

113

BURGIN: Which works of his do you admire?

BORGES: Well, his book on *Don Quixote* and his essays.

BURGIN:
So you think he's a good thinker, I mean, apart from his writing?

BORGES:
Oh, he is definitely, yes, a great mind. What I said against Unamuno is that he is interested in things that I am not interested in. He is very worried about his personal immortality. He says, "I want to go on being Miguel De Unamuno." Well, I don't want to go on being Jorge Luis Borges. In fact, I have uttered the wish that if I am born again I will have no personal memories of my other life. I mean to say, I don't want to go on being Jorge Luis Borges, I want to forget all about him. But that, of course, those are merely personal differences. You might as well say that I like coffee and he likes tea, or that I like plains and he prefers the mountains, no?

BURGIN:
"The opinions of an author are wrought by the superficial accidents of circumstance," that's what you said.

BORGES: Yes, quite right, that's what I said, yes.

BURGIN:
Do you enjoy any other arts outside of literature? I know you're not passionately involved in them as you are in literature. But what other arts do you enjoy?

BORGES:
For example, when I wrote with Bioy Casares, his wife was always putting on gramophone records. And then, after

114

a time, we felt all that music that was going on—it was a very large house—in a distant room. There was one kind of music that we enjoyed, that stimulated us and made us, perhaps, write better. And then we told her and she tried several experiments and we found out that when Debussy was on it did us no good, Ravel did us no good either, Bach left us untouched. But when she tried Brahms, it turned out that Brahms was our music, no?

BURGIN: Would you like Mahler then?

BORGES: Gustav Mahler. I never heard him.

BURGIN: Stravinsky. Have you ever heard him?

BORGES:
Stravinsky. I heard him once in a concert, and I felt as if I were intoxicated, eh? I felt so happy about it, I felt so happy that I never tried to repeat that experience, because I thought I might be baffled and disappointed.

BURGIN: What was the piece? Do you remember?

BORGES:
I don't know. I was in the centre of the Republic, there were two or three professors that had been lecturing and they asked me if I would go to a concert with them. Then I said, "Well, look here, I'll go with you because I enjoy your company, but I don't think I'll enjoy the music because I'm very very ignorant." They said, "Well, if you don't care about it, just walk away, you don't have to stand it." Then I went and suddenly I felt a kind of dizziness and happiness coming over me and when we walked out we all felt very, very friendly, and we patted each other on the shoulder and we laughed for no reason at all and it was Stravinsky.

115

BURGIN:

You love painting and architecture, don't you? I mean your stories seem to me very vivid visually.

BORGES:

Are they really visual, or does the visibility come from Chesterton?

BURGIN:

You seem to have that ability to make a purely imagined world, such as the city of the immortals, come to life.

BORGES: I wonder if they really come to life?

BURGIN: For me they do. I can only speak for myself.

BORGES:

Yes, of course. Now my sister paints. She's a very fine painter.

BURGIN: What style does she paint in?

BORGES:

She's always painting, well, large gardens and old-fashioned pink houses or if not those, angels, but angels who are musicians. She's a very unobtrusive painter. For example, well, she studies perspective drawing and so on. But people who know little or nothing about painting think of her paintings as being just scrawls done by a child. Then, of course, there are painters who have struck me, for example, Turner, Rembrandt, or Titian.

BURGIN:

Have you ever seen anything by the Dutch graphic artist, M. C. Escher?

116

BORGES: No, I haven't.

BURGIN:

He's a contemporary of yours, born around the same time, and strangely his work in visual terms alludes to some of your favourite themes and subjects. I mean he has pictures about infinity and alternative realities, and so forth.

BORGES:

No, I haven't. But I'm very fond of the engravings of Dürer. At home I have a very large engraving of his "Night, Death and The Devil." And I'm fond of Turner also and perhaps of the English or Flemish landscape painters. I rather dislike El Greco, perhaps because I think that he never painted an intelligent face, no? All the characters, let's say, in the pictures of El Greco seem to be, somehow, cocksure, stubborn, or rather stupid, no? I don't think one would have carried on a conversation with them.

6

DARWIN; NIETZSCHE; EXISTENTIALISM AND
SARTRE; FREUD; SYMMETRIES; THE
PATTERNS OF COINCIDENCE;
TOLERANCE AND SCEPTICISM; PERÓN. . . .

BURGIN:

I wanted to ask you a few questions about some philosophers.

BORGES: I'm very ignorant of it. Well, go on.

BURGIN:

I wanted to ask you about some of the philosophers you
haven't mentioned so much in your work, because you
have mentioned many.

BORGES:

The amount I haven't mentioned is far beyond the amount
I have mentioned, no? But I would like to say that I was
always very interested in philosophy, yet I've done more
rereading than reading. Because I find that I get more
out of rereading an old book than out of reading a new
one. I've done that on principle. I've always thought that
in the Middle Ages people were very lucky because they
had few books but those books were essential. Of course,
nowadays, there's so much written about books that one
hardly finds one's way through to the books.

BURGIN:

I wanted to ask you about Darwin and the theories of

118

evolution—whether that has influenced your writing or your thought at all.

BORGES:

As a matter of fact, I don't think it has. I read *The Origin of Species.*

BURGIN: And you weren't impressed?

BORGES:

No, I was impressed but, well, what happens to Darwin is that the argument is fairly simple—of course, it's filled out by examples and illustrations—but once you get the drift of it, you don't want to go on reading, because you are more or less convinced, no? At least, I was quite young, I felt convinced by it. I felt that what Darwin was saying was true, but he's not a very charming writer, no? It's not that I'm against Darwin.

In fact, I don't think I've ever been asked about Darwin. I don't see the connection. Now of course, I've done some reading on evolution, but on the whole, I would rather be on Samuel Butler's or on Shaw's side than on Darwin's. Because in Butler and in Shaw, the stress is on the will, no? But in the case of Darwin, as far as I can recall it, the idea is that evolution happens in a kind of haphazard way, no? I mean, well, the survival of the fittest and all that.

BURGIN:

Well, speaking about the will, I have the feeling that you aren't too fond of Nietzsche as a thinker.

BORGES:

No. Well, I think that I am unfair to Nietzsche, because though I have read and reread many of his books, well, I think that if you omit *Thus Spoke Zarathustra*, if you omit that book—a kind of sham Bible, no?—I mean a sham biblical style—but if you omit that book you get very interesting books.

BURGIN: *Beyond Good and Evil.*

BORGES:

Yes, I've read them in German. And I greatly enjoyed them. But yet, somehow, I have never felt any sympathy for him as a man, no? I mean I feel a great sympathy for Schopenhauer, or for ever so many writers, but in the case of Nietzsche I feel there is something hard and I won't say priggish, I mean as a person he has no modesty about him. The same thing happens to me with Blake. I don't like writers who are making sweeping statements all the time. Of course, you might argue that what I'm saying is a sweeping statement also, no? Well, one has to say things with a certain emphasis.

BURGIN:

Don't you feel, though, in the case of Nietzsche, he might be somewhat akin to Whitman? In that the personae of their works are quite different from the actual men behind them?

BORGES:

Yes, but in the case of Whitman he gives you a very attractive persona. In the case of Nietzsche he gives you a very disagreeable one, at least to me. I feel I can sympathize with Whitman, but I can hardly sympathize with Nietzsche. In fact, I don't suppose he wanted people to sympathize with him.

BURGIN:

Have you done much reading in political philosophy?

BORGES:

No. Not at all. Because, you see, my father was an anarchist in the Spencerian sense of the word, no? I mean an individual against the state. And I've met some of the anarchists, and I've never felt any sympathy with socialism. No, I'm very ignorant of these things.

BURGIN: About politics?

BORGES:

Yes, very, very ignorant. I mean, as to my political opinions, I don't think I could convince anybody of them. But I've made it pretty clear, for example, where I stand. People have known all along that I was, let's say, against Hitler, against anti-Semitism, against Fascism, against Communism, against our own dictator, Perón.

BURGIN: What repulsed you about Communism?

BORGES:

Well, because I have been brought up to think that the individual should be strong and the state should be weak. I couldn't be enthusiastic about theories where the state is more important than the individual. Now, I'm a conservative, but being a conservative in my country doesn't mean being a diehard; being a conservative means being, let's say, a mild liberal. If you are a conservative in the Argentine, nobody thinks of you as being a fascist or as being a nationalist. On the contrary, to tell you the truth, I think being a conservative in the Argentine means being rather sceptical in political matters, and disbelieving in any violent changes. That's what it boils down to, but, of course, here I think the word "conservative" means something else. Now take the word "radical"—in my country, radical stands, let's say, for a kind of halfway house, middle left, though, of course, they're more

121

demagogues than the conservatives who are not demagogues at all, no? You see, if you take those words in all countries, they mean different things. A radical in Buenos Aires is, more or less, like a Republican or a conservative here. But I suppose, if you say *here* that somebody is a radical, you think of him as a radical revolutionary, no? And, of course, those meanings change, they change with history, they change with time. So that being a radical in 1890 is quite different from what it is today in Buenos Aires, no?

BURGIN:

Of course, you've also said that our opinions are the accidents of chance so that in a sense, this must seem trivial to you.

BORGES:

Well, no, but what I said, and I've tried to make that clear even at the cost of repeating myself, which I'm doing all the time, is that I don't think a writer should be judged by his opinions, by his political opinions. Or even by his religious opinions because those opinions may be on the surface, no? I suppose if you had asked Cervantes what he was, he would have said, "Well, I'm a Roman Catholic, I'm a Catholic, of course." Had you asked Quevedo what he was, he would have said, "I'm a Catholic." But the words would mean different things because they were said by different men. Because I suppose that though Cervantes was a Catholic, and a good Catholic, you feel that he's full of tolerance. When you read *Don Quixote*, you cannot think of that man as sending anybody to the stake. Of course, it has been said that he had no word against the Inquisition, but he couldn't have had a word against the Inquisition because he would have been risking his own life. So that when Cervantes said, "I am a Catholic," he was sincere. When Quevedo

122

said, "I am a Catholic," he was also sincere, and yet, the meaning behind the words is quite different because Quevedo was a fanatic and Cervantes evidently wasn't. When you read *Don Quixote* you cannot think of the man who wrote that story as being very cocksure of his own opinion, or that he could burn people, or execute people for having a different opinion.

I'm thinking of another particular case now. I think it very unfair that Kipling should be judged by his political opinions, because though I think that the British Empire can't be defended—I'm not prepared to defend it—but I think that you might not care about the British Empire or that you might think that in the long run it didn't make for good, and yet you may think of Kipling as a very fine writer. I'm sure he was. And in the case of Whitman, well, I think Whitman is different, because I suppose if you're against democracy, I wonder if you can accept Walt Whitman. Well, I suppose you can accept many of his images. I suppose you can. The reader wouldn't be biased against them, no?

BURGIN:

Well, take the case of Wagner. His music was used as a theme for the Nazis, and so many people refuse to listen to him now, or are repulsed by him. Yet if people can consider music as an entity in itself, then they can still appreciate and enjoy his music.

BORGES:

Well, I'm very ignorant about music, but I can hardly think of music as having opinions. In fact, I think of music as being beyond opinions. I remember a very fine and very deep statement of Schopenhauer's. Schopenhauer said that he could imagine music as being a world in itself. Of course, it's no good saying that music cannot be a world in itself because in order to exist it needs composers and musicians and instruments, pianos and fiddles. That's not the point, that's what we're supposed to be making from the idea of music. But you might imagine a world of music, no?

BURGIN:
I was wondering, if we could get back to philosophy, what figures from the twentieth century you admire, if any.

BORGES:
No, no, I admire, yes—but that doesn't mean that...

BURGIN: You follow them.

BORGES:
No. But I would think of Bergson. And, do you think of William James as belonging to the twentieth or to the nineteenth century? To the twentieth, no? Highly contemporary. Well, look here, I've read and reread and I found it very stimulating and very interesting and I've taken many of my pet subjects from him—I'm speaking of Bertrand Russell. Now as to the existentialists, I've tried, well, I don't think I could really like them and yet Sartre has been very kind to me, personally, I mean in his magazine he wrote about me. When I met him in Paris, I suppose he knew that we stood on different ground, but, of course, we tried to get on together and we did, but somehow I never felt any sympathy for his philosophy. I never had any sympathy for a pathetic philosophy, no? And the philosophers of existentialism harping on personal matters, or Unamuno being so worried about his own immortality and saying that God, after all, is for the producing or making of immortality and that if God doesn't make him immortal, he has no use for God, I never could understand that. In fact, in two or three sonnets I have uttered the wish that I might die, and that if I'm reborn again, I would like to be

reborn without a personal memory, at least without a memory of this life. . . . And I have tried to read Kierkegaard. I have always felt repelled by him. Unamuno, I think of him as a very important writer, but I have no sympathy with him.

BURGIN: What about Heidegger?

BORGES:

No. Heidegger writes in abominable German, I should say. When I knew that he was on the side of the Nazis, I felt very glad, no? I said, well, that's as it should be, no? But of course, I know I'm being very old-fashioned saying these things.

BURGIN:

Do you think existentialism could have a harmful effect on men?

BORGES:

I think that existentialism makes for a kind of vanity. I met Sartre and he praised me up. Naturally, it's a great thing for an Argentine to be praised by a Frenchman, no? But I always disliked him.

BURGIN: Personally, you mean?

BORGES:

No, no, no, no. I dislike people who are out for propaganda. I don't think he should have allowed a cafe to be called Café Existentialism. I don't think of Bishop Berkeley doing that kind of thing, or of Schopenhauer. And I could hardly think of him as a gentleman, though, of course, that's another old-fashioned word, no?

BURGIN: Unfortunately.

125

BORGES:

Unfortunately, yes. I think that the species is dying out, or has died out. It's a great pity.

BURGIN:

I take it you don't think much of Freud, either.

BORGES:

No, I always disliked him. But I've always been a great reader of Jung. I read Jung in the same way as, let's say, I might read Pliny or Frazer's *Golden Bough*, I read it as a kind of mythology, or as a kind of museum or encyclopaedia of curious lores.

BURGIN:

When you say that you dislike Freud, what do you mean?

BORGES:

I think of him as a kind of madman, no? A man labouring over a sexual obsession. Well, perhaps he didn't take it to heart. Perhaps he was just doing it as a kind of game. I tried to read him, and I thought of him either as a charlatan or as a madman, in a sense. After all, the world is far too complex to be boiled down to that all-too simple scheme. But in Jung, well, of course, Jung I have read far more widely than Freud, but in Jung you feel a wide and hospitable mind. In the case of Freud, it all boils down to a few rather unpleasant facts. But, of course, that's merely my ignorance or my bias.

BURGIN: You've said "reality favours symmetry."

BORGES: Ah yes, it's true.

BURGIN:

When you say that, does it come out of your own experience?

BORGES:

Yes, or perhaps because I'm on the lookout for symmetries.

BURGIN:

You've criticized yourself before for always looking for the symmetries, the mirrors, the labyrinths in life. Do you really feel that way or . . .

BORGES:

No, no, I feel that way. But perhaps coincidences are given to us that would involve the idea of a secret plan, no? Coincidences are given to us so that we may feel there is a pattern—that there is a pattern in life, that things mean something. Of course, there is a pattern in the sense that we have night and day, the four seasons, being born, living and dying, the stars and so on, but there may be a more subtle kind of pattern, no?

BURGIN: Within each individual's life.

BORGES:

Yes, within each individual's life, because I find so many coincidences. Of course, as many things happen, coincidences are bound to happen also, but I find very strange coincidences and they are of no use whatever to me except for the fact that they leave a pattern. For example, Bioy Casares and I were working on a translation of Sir Thomas Browne. That translation never found its way into print, because the editors said there was no interest in that and forgot all about it. Now we found a sentence in Sir Thomas Browne in Spanish, "defiéndeme Dios de mí." Only he made a mistake and he wrote "defiéndeme Dios de me." Now where else could he have got that from? Well, of course, we corrected the mistake and wrote "defiédeme Dios de mí."

127

A day or so later, I went to Mitchell's Book Store in Buenos Aires, well it's no longer there, and in the basement I found a new translation of Montaigne into English. I opened one of the volumes at random and there I found "defiéndeme Dios mí," and with the same misprint, "de me." The editor, of course he had no Spanish, he thought that Montaigne knew all about it. And then, as I knew that Sir Thomas Browne had been a close reader of Montaigne, there was the clue I had been looking for. He had found that quotation in Montaigne, and the proof lay in the misprint, no?

Well, I felt greatly elated at the discovery and I went that night to see Bioy Casares and I had jotted down where the edition of Montaigne might be found. And we were working over an anthology of Spanish verse. He had those books of Rivadeneyra in a collection, he had a pile of them on the table. While I was talking to him, he opened one of books, and there he found a poem of Cristóbal de Castillejo, Garcilaso's enemy, glossing the line "defiéndeme Dios de mí." I said, "Look here, I found it in Montaigne this morning." We would have had to have examined thousands of volumes in thousands of years and perhaps never found out these things. And then we felt very proud. Of course, we wrote a short note (in the translation), saying Sir Thomas Browne took his quotation from essay number so and so of Montaigne where the same misprint is found and so on.

BURGIN: You're very close friends with Casares, aren't you?

BORGES:

Oh yes, my best friend. I go to see him every night in Buenos Aires. You see, there you had a coincidence, and the coincidence was of no use whatever.

BURGIN:

He must be close to you in his concerns and interests.

BORGES:

Yes, yes, but he's a better writer than I am. Well, he's a younger man. But it's very strange because I'm sixty-eight and he should be, I suppose, nearing fifty, and yet he has influenced me far more than I have influenced him. He has taught me many things. And I may have taught him, I may have led him to the reading of some authors or others. I sent him to Stevenson and he sent me to Doctor Johnson, and so on.

BURGIN: Does he write novels?

BORGES:

He writes novels and tales. Very fine. Always with a touch of the fantastic. And then we collaborate, under the name H. Bustos Domecq. That's because my great-great-grand-father had the name Bustos and Domecq was a French fore-father of Bioy. Because that kind of name is quite com-mon in Buenos Aires, Bustos Domecq, no? It doesn't sound odd. Here it may be a bit of a fancy name, but in Buenos Aires, it's the kind of name that you might expect.

BURGIN:

Have you ever tried to collaborate with any other writers?

BORGES:

Yes, but I failed. It didn't work because we were thinking of ourselves as two different men. If you collaborate, you have to forget you have an identity. If you are to work successfully in collaboration, you shouldn't think whether you said that or whether I said it. I mean you have an idea, then you have another. But if you think of something and that thing is wrong, or if you are too polite and accept what the other chap says, or if, on the contrary, you have a feeling of vanity and don't like having your hints rejected, then collaboration is impossible.

129

BURGIN:

Do artists stick together in Buenos Aires? Is there any kind of community of artists?

BORGES:

No. No. There were literary meetings and so on, but that was quite some time ago. Nowadays there is a Sociedad de Argentina Escritor, but that is rather a kind of trades union, no?

BURGIN: There's no real fellowship, no real community.

BORGES:

No, but I think that's to the good, eh? Well, perhaps when a young man knows that he's a writer, he should be meeting other writers and discussing things with them. But afterwards you don't need that, because you know your own limits, you know your possibilities, and you don't have to go over them. But I think it's very stimulating for a young writer to be able to talk literature.

BURGIN: But you were involved in the Ultraista.*

BORGES: That was a kind of sham, the whole thing.

BURGIN:

At the time, though, it meant something to you, didn't it?

BORGES:

No, no. We all knew it was a kind of joke, we never took it seriously, but we enjoyed meeting each other, we enjoyed our friendship. Now as to the manifestos and all those things—"the one elementary fact about literature is the

* Roughly the equivalent of German Expressionism, the movement was active in Spain during the early 1920s.

metaphor"—we might as well have said that the one elementary fact about literature is the semicolon or the full stop, no?

BURGIN:

What about the people of Buenos Aires as a whole? Is there a sense of community among them? How are they reacting to their government? Is there a sense of patriotism, or something that's binding them together?

BORGES:

I think that we all think the government means well, that they are honest men. Now that may not be saying too much in this country, but in our country, if we feel that the men who are in power are gentlemen and that they are not stuffing their pockets with public money, well, we should be grateful for that, as there are so many scoundrels. . . .

BURGIN:

You said once that Argentinians are very sceptical by nature.

BORGES:

Yes, yes, they are sceptical about the government also. But I think that scepticism makes for good because without it we'd be having revolutions all the time. But if you're really sceptical, you'll say, "Well, this isn't a very good government after all, but perhaps if we had another it would be still worse, it might be as bad as this."

BURGIN: Do you think of yourself as a sceptic?

BORGES: I wonder, eh?

BURGIN: You're sceptical about ultimate values.

BORGES: Yes.

BURGIN: But you always try to affirm the dignity of the artist.

BORGES:
Quite so. I think that the writer is—of course, it's very difficult for a writer to explain himself—but yet the mere fact that I enjoy reading, that I enjoy writing, that there are people who enjoy what I write, that should be sufficient I think. I don't think any other justification is needed, don't you think so?

BURGIN: Yes, I really do.

BORGES:
But people think that, after all, a writer should think of himself politically, well, we've spoken about this. I think that writing is far too mysterious to be governed by that. . . . Now I wonder, suppose you had to teach English literature and you had to choose one writer . . .

BURGIN: Well, Shakespeare.

BORGES: No, perhaps Coleridge might be better.

BURGIN: Than Shakespeare?

BORGES:
Because, if you have Coleridge, then Shakespeare might be worked in. I suppose the wisest thing to do would be to choose a quite recent author and then you could trace back the different trends, don't you think so?

BURGIN:
It's an interesting idea. Of course, as you say, every time you write something new you write or rewrite something old, every time you read something new, you reread something old.

BORGES:

Well, I mean, if you're speaking of Emerson, you're looking back on a very long tradition. Now in the case of Scott Fitzgerald, I don't think you're doing that kind of thing. I don't think you're looking back on a long tradition or on a very important tradition.

BURGIN:

Then you think that any writer whose work endures and seems to have universal impact or importance will be part of a tradition, will be part of a continuum. You think of literature not as something with demarcations, with periods that begin and end, but as something fluid.

BORGES:

Yes, that's true, yes. That's why the whole idea of teaching, for example, Argentine literature, is rubbish. In the case of Argentine literature, especially so. Because how can you think of Argentine literature outside the Spanish language? How can you think of it outside the influence of French markets. It can't be done. You can't speak of Chaucer without thinking about the Italians and the French. It can't be done. Meaningless. And you can't speak about Baudelaire without going back to De Quincey and to Edgar Allan Poe. You can't speak of them without going back to somebody else. Perhaps comparative literature is the only sensible thing.

BURGIN:

What about a writer like Swift though? Can you really think that he belonged to a tradition?

BORGES:

Swift is a very curious case, eh? Such an original writer.

BURGIN: I imagine you must really love *Gulliver's Travels*.

BORGES:

Especially the last chapters, no? But those chapters are generally left out. I mean the stories about the Yahoos and the Island of Laputa. But how strange his satire on science, because nowadays if we write against science, it's because we think of it as an evil. We think of it as a powerful foe. But he was a very intelligent man, a man of genius, and yet he thought of science as being a futility. I mean he was poking fun at the scientists, not because he thought of them as a danger, but because he thought that they were fools and they were trifling their time away, no? Isn't that strange? And yet he was a very intelligent man, and committed that mistake. Because he thought that all those people working away in their laboratories and so on were mere fools. And Bacon had the same feeling about astronomy. He was all for science, for the delicate study of things, the study of nature and so on, but he thought that astronomy was useless because, after all, you have no use for what is happening in the sky. This should be a lesson of humility to us, no? I mean if two such men as Swift and Bacon went astray . . . on the contrary, then we can make our own mistakes and be quite cheerful about them.

BURGIN: Have you corresponded much with other writers?

BORGES: No.

BURGIN: I didn't think you had. You've been more solitary.

BORGES:

And besides, I'm a very poor letter writer. For example, I'm awfully fond of my mother. I love her. I'm always thinking about her. And, of course, I have to dictate my letters. But even when, for example, while I am away from her, I always send her very very trivial letters. Because somehow I feel that she knows what I am feeling and that

134

I have no need to say anything, that I can just be trivial and cheerful and commonplace and that she will know exactly how I am feeling. So that the letters I send her—sometimes they are even postcards to help me out—I suppose they are quite meaningless to anybody else, and yet there is a kind of secret writing between us, although we've never spoken about it. She knows me and I know her. I think that I might spend six months without a letter from her and if I knew that she was well, I wouldn't be worried about it. And she would feel much the same way about me. Of course, I might be worried because she might be ailing or something might have happened to her. But if I know from all sources that she's getting on, I don't have to worry about what she says, and she doesn't have to worry about what I say.

BURGIN: She must be a remarkable woman.

BORGES:
She *is* a remarkable woman. She was in prison in Perón's time. My sister also.

BURGIN: Perón put them in prison?

BORGES:
Yes. My sister, well, of course, in the case of my mother it was different, because she was already an old lady—she's ninety-one now—and so her prison was her own home, no? But my sister was sent with some friends of hers to a jail for prostitutes in order to insult her. Then, she somehow smuggled a letter to us, I don't know how she managed it, saying that the prison was such a lovely place, that everybody was so kind, that being in prison was so restful, that it had a beautiful patio, black and white like a chessboard. In fact, she worded it so that we thought she was in some awful dungeon, no? Of course, what she really wanted was

135

for us to feel, well, not to worry so much about her. She kept on saying what nice people there were, and how being in jail was much better than having to go out to cocktails or parties and so on. She was in prison with other ladies, and the other ladies told me that they felt awful about it. But my sister just said the Lord's Prayer. There were eleven of them in the same room, and my sister said her prayers, then she went to sleep immediately. All the time she was in jail, she didn't know how long a time might pass before she would see her husband, her children, and her mother or me. And afterwards she told me—but this was when she was out of jail—she said that, after all, my grandfather died for this country, my great-grandfather fought the Spaniards. They all did what they could for the country. And I, by the mere fact of being in prison, I was doing something also. So this is as it should be.

BURGIN: How long was she in prison?

BORGES:
A month. Of course they told her that if she wrote a letter she would be free at once. And the same thing happened to my mother and my sister, her friends and my mother answered the same thing. They said, "If you write a letter to the Señora you'll get out." "What señora are you talking about?" "This señora is Señora Perón." "Well, as we don't know her, and she doesn't know us, it's quite meaningless for us to write to her." But what they really wanted was that those ladies would write a letter and then they would publish it, no? And then people would say how merciful Perón was, and how we were free now. The whole thing was a kind of trick, it *was* a trick. But they saw through it. That was the kind of thing they had to undergo at the time.

BURGIN: It was a horrible time.

136

BORGES:

Oh, it was. For example, when you have a toothache, when you have to go to the dentist, the first thing that you think about when you wake up is the whole ordeal, but during some ten years, of course, I had my personal grievances too, but in those ten years the first thing I thought about when I was awake was, well, "Perón is in power."

BURGIN:

What was he like as a man? Was he like a baby Hitler?

BORGES: No, but Hitler was a brave man.

BURGIN: A crazy man.

BORGES:

Yes, but a brave man. Perón was a coward. Besides, I think Hitler believed in himself and Perón didn't. Perón knew he was a humbug. And all his henchmen knew he was a humbug. They were all out for loot. Very different. Hitler was a man of action. He fought, he died, he inspired men. I hated him, but I thought of him, perhaps, as a crazy man but as a man who was in a sense respectable. In the case of Perón, Perón was more like Mussolini. Though Mussolini was far more intelligent than Perón. Perón was a humbug, and he knew it, and everybody knew it. But Perón could be very cruel. I mean he had people tortured, killed. And his wife was a common prostitute. She had a brothel near Junín. And that must have embittered him, no? I mean, if a girl is a whore in a large city that doesn't mean too much; but in a small town in the pampas, everybody knows everybody else. And being one of the whores is like being the barber or the surgeon. And that must have greatly embittered her. To be known and to be despised by everybody and to be used.

137

7

LITERATURE AS PLEASURE; *THE MAKER*;
THE LITERATURE OF LITERATURE; A
CHANGE IN DIRECTION; *DON QUIXOTE* and
CERVANTES; HIROSHIMA; DEATH AND THE
PROBLEM OF INFINITY;
DISSOLVING REALITY....

BURGIN:
You know, I was thinking of how, during all our talks,
you have often emphasized enjoyment, that one should
primarily enjoy literature. Do you think pleasure is the
main purpose of literature, if it can be said to have a
purpose?

BORGES:
Well, pleasure, I don't know, but you should get a kick out
of it, no?

BURGIN: Yes.

BORGES:
Well, if you allow me to attempt slang, yes, I think that
should be so. You know I'm a professor of English and
American literature and tell my students that if you begin a
book, if at the end of fifteen or twenty pages you feel that
the book is a task for you, then, lay that book and lay that
author aside for a time because it won't do you any good.
For example, one of my favourite authors is De Quincey.
Well, as he's a rather slow-moving author, people somehow

138

don't like him. So I say, well, if you don't like De Quincey then let him alone, my task is not to impose my likes or dislikes on you. What I really want is that you should fall in love with American or English literature, and if you find your way to a few authors or a few authors find their way to you, then that's as it should be. You don't have to worry about dates. And I should advise you to read the book, to read the foreword if you care to, and then you might read an article or so in any old edition of the *Encyclopaedia Britannica*, because the new ones are no good, no? And then take any history of English literature, it might be Andrew Lang, it might be Saintsbury, though I'm not overfond of him, it might be Sampson, though he's intruding his likes and dislikes, but I would say any of those three, though Andrew Lang stops at Swinburne, from Beowulf to Swinburne. Now as to American histories of literature, there's a very amusing book by a man called Lewisohn.

BURGIN: Ludwig Lewisohn?

BORGES:

Yes, but of course, his work is based on psychoanalysis and I wonder if you can psychoanalyse Edgar Allan Poe or Nathaniel Hawthorne and Jonathan Edwards, no? I think it's rather late in the day. And if you were a contemporary, it would be far more difficult because you'd have too many facts about them. It's a pity, no, that that whole book is based on what seems to me a wrong approach?

And as I say, as to examinations, I won't ask you the dates of an author because then you would ask me and then I would fail. But, of course, I think it's all to the good that you should think of Dr. Johnson as belonging to the eighteenth century and of Milton belonging to the seventeenth, because if not, then you couldn't understand them. Now, as to those birth dates, that may or may not be important. As to the dates of their deaths, as they didn't know

139

them themselves, why should you know them? Why should you know more than the authors did? And as to articles, bibliographies and so on, you don't have to worry about that. What you have to do is to read the authors. Then, as to histories of literature, they are all more or less copies of one another, with variations.

BURGIN:

If enjoyment is paramount, then what do you suppose it is that gives one a sense of enjoyment from a book?

BORGES:

There may be two opposite explanations to that. The individual is getting away from his personal circumstances and finding his way into another world, but at the same time, perhaps that other world interests him because it's nearer his inner self than his circumstances. I mean if I, suppose I take one of my favourite authors, Stevenson, if I were to read Stevenson now, I would feel that as I was reading the book I wouldn't think of myself as being in England or in South America. I would think I was inside the book. And yet that book might be telling me a secret, or half-guessed-at things about myself. But, of course, those explanations go together, no? If you accept one, you don't have to refuse the other.

BURGIN:

Of all the books you've published, do you have a favourite book?

BORGES:

Of all my books, yes. The book called *The Maker, El Hacedor*. Yes, because it wrote itself. And my English translator, or my American translator, he wrote to me and said that there was no English word for "El Hacedor." And then I wrote him back, saying that "El Hacedor" had been translated from the English "The Maker." But, of course, all words in a foreign tongue have a certain distinction behind them, no? So that "El Hacedor" meant more to him than "The Maker." But when I used "El Hacedor" for the poet, for Homer, I was merely translating the Old English or the Middle English word "maker."

BURGIN:

Some people didn't take you seriously when you said that *El Hacedor*, translated back into English as *Dream Tigers*, would make all your other books unnecessary. But as I read it, I think more and more that perhaps it was more than a joke on your part—saying that.

BORGES:

Well, I know, because the book seems to be slight, but it isn't really slight.

BURGIN:

It has all your essential themes and motifs and, more important, your voice.

BORGES:

The book may be a slight book, but it isn't a slight book to me, because when I go back to that book, I find that I've said the things I had to say or that I worked out the images I had to work out. And besides, the book has found some favour with the public. It's not a boring book. In fact, it couldn't be because it's so short.

BURGIN:

When were the poems that were in that collection written?

BORGES:

They were written all through my life. My editor told me, "We want a new book from you, there should be a market for that book." And I said, "I haven't any book." And then my editor said to me, "Oh yes, you have. If you go through your shelves or drawers you'll find odds and ends. Maybe a book can be evolved from them." So I think I remember it was a rainy Sunday in Buenos Aires and I had nothing whatever to do because, well, there was an appointment that had failed. I had my sight, I wasn't blind, so I thought, I'll look over my papers. Maybe I'll find something in my drawers. I found cuttings, old magazines, and then I found that there was the book all ready for me.

BURGIN:

Of pieces that you had thought were insignificant before?

BORGES:

Yes, and I took them to the editor and said, "I want you to tell me honestly, you don't have to answer me today or next week, whether you think this book, this kind of crazy-quilt patchwork, can be published, you take ten days or a fortnight or a month over it, and look it over carefully because I don't want you to be spending money on a book that nobody will buy or that may find some very hard critics." And then he answered me within a week, saying "Yes."

BURGIN:

I wanted to ask you about one of your parables in *El Hacedor*, your parable about Cervantes.

BORGES:

Ah yes! I'm very interested in Cervantes. I think, I wonder how you feel about it, when I think of English literature I'm attracted to it, among many other things, because when I'm thinking of it, I'm thinking about men more than about books. I think that English literature, like England, is very personal. For example, if I think of Sir Thomas Browne or Doctor Johnson, George Bernard Shaw or John Bunyan,

142

or the men who wrote the Saxon Elegies, I think of them as *men* even as I might think of the many characters in Dickens or in Shakespeare. While I get the sense, of course I may be wrong, I get the sense that when I'm thinking about Spanish literature, I'm thinking about books rather than about men. Really, because of my ignorance, I'm attracted to Cervantes even as I'm attracted to Dickens and Shaw—because I can imagine him. But in the case of other writers, I can hardly imagine them, I think of their books. I wonder, for example, had I the chance to talk to Lope de Vega, I wonder what we would have spoken about.

BURGIN:

He wrote eighteen hundred plays, or something like that.

BORGES:

Yes, I would think of his plays rather. While if somebody said, "You'll be having supper with Sir Thomas Browne, or even with Doctor Johnson"—of course, he would have been full of sweeping statements—I would have said, "I'll enjoy this evening, I can imagine it." Well, Cervantes is one of the few Spanish authors I can imagine. I know more or less, what a chat with him would be. I know, for example, how he might apologize for some of the things he's written. How he wouldn't take himself too seriously. I'm sure of it, even as in the case of Samuel Butler or Wells, so one of the reasons why I feel attracted to Cervantes is that I think of him not only as a writer, one of the greatest of novelists, but also as a man. And as Whitman says, "Camerado, this is no book, Who touches this touches a man." But I hardly ever get that feeling with Spanish books, or with Italian books. But I get that feeling, I get it all the time, when I'm reading American or English literature.

BURGIN:

But now, I'm curious, you have this parable of Cervantes,

and you have written other parables about Dante and
Homer and Shakespeare; I was wondering how you got the
idea, because I don't know of any other writer who has
ever done this. I mean, to have written parables in which
you tried to imagine or re-imagine the history of particular compositions or of their authors' lives or destinies?

BORGES:

I think the explanation is fairly simple. The explanation is
that I am interested in literature, not only for its own sake,
but also as one of the many destinies of man. I mean, as I
am interested in soldiers and in adventurers and in mystics
—well, I come from a military family and so on—I am also
interested in literary men. I mean, in the fact of a man
dedicating himself to his dreams, then trying to work them
out. And doing his best to make other people share them.
I'm interested in literary life. Of course, I'm not the first
writer to do that because there are many Henry James
stories about literary subject, about literary men.

BURGIN:

You've really based your whole literature on literature
itself in a way.

BORGES:

Yes. That may be an argument against my literature, and
yet why? In many of my stories and poems the central
character is a literary man. Well, this means to say that I
think that literature has not only enriched the world by
giving it books but also by evolving a new type of man, the
man of letters. For example, you might not care for the
works of Coleridge, you might think that outside of three
or four poems, "The Ancient Mariner," "Christabel,"
"Kubla Khan," maybe "Time, River, and Imagining," what
he wrote is not very interesting, it's very wordy, and very
perplexed and perplexing stuff, confused and confusing stuff

144

and yet I'm sure that you think of Coleridge as you might think of somebody you had known, no? I mean, that though his writing is sometimes rather unreal, yet you think of him as being a real man—perhaps because of his unreality also, and because he lived in a kind of haze world or dream world, no? So that I think literature has enriched the world not only through books, but through a new type of man, the man of letters.

BURGIN:

Have you ever tried writing in a more realistic way, basing your stories not on literature but on developed characters and . . .

BORGES: Yes. I have done that.

BURGIN: You did try that first?

BORGES:

No, no. I'm going back to that. I wonder if you've seen the last edition of *El Apeph*?

BURGIN:

"La Intrusa," yes, that's a very atypical story of yours in some ways. But in some ways it isn't.

BORGES:

No, but I find that "La Intrusa" is a different story from the others. Well, I have several plots of the same kind and when I'm back in Buenos Aires, I'll go on with them.

BURGIN: Why do you suppose you've changed your direction?

BORGES:

Well, there might be many reasons. I suppose the real reason is that when I thought of "La Intrusa" I was very

145

interested in it and I wrote it down in quite a short time. That might be a reason. And the other reason might be that I feel that the kind of stories you get in *El Aleph* and in *Ficciones* are becoming rather mechanical, and that people expect that kind of thing from me. So that I feel as if I were a kind of high fidelity, a kind of gadget, no? A kind of factory producing stories about mistaken identity, about mazes, about tigers, about mirrors, about people being somebody else, or about all men being the same man or one man being his own mortal foe. And another reason, that may be a rather malicious one, is that there are quite a few people all over the world who are writing that kind of story and there's no reason why I should go on doing it. Especially as some of them do it far better than I do, no?

BURGIN:

Well, they followed you, and no, I don't think they do it better or as well. Though, of course, some of your stories, like "The Form of the Sword," are more "realistic."

BORGES:

That's one of the stories I like least, because it's a trick story after all. Now a friend of mine told me that he saw through the trick, and I thought that is as it should be because I did think of the story as a trick story. I thought that if the reader felt that the man was talking about himself, it would make the whole thing more pathetic, but if he were merely telling a story about somebody who betrayed him, then that's a mere episode. But if a traitor in a bashful way found that the only way of telling the story was to think of himself as outside the story, or rather, joining together with the central character, the story might be better and besides it might be said for the story that, well, let's suppose—let's suppose you made me some confession about yourself, no? You told me something that nobody knew or that nobody was supposed to know, or that you wanted

146

hidden and suppose that in the moment you were telling it to me, you felt outside the whole thing because the mere fact of telling it made you the teller and not the told.

BURGIN:

I think you underrate that story because, though, as you say, it ends in a trick, an O. Henry kind of reversal, I think that . . .

BORGES:

But of course, when I wrote that story I was quite young and then I believed in cleverness, and now I think that cleverness is a hindrance. I don't think a writer should be clever, or clever in a mechanical way, no?

BURGIN:

I think it's deeper than the plot. I think it's thematically very interesting and I think it's somewhat akin to that story "The Theologians" because . . .

BORGES: No. "The Theologians" is a better story.

BURGIN: "The Theologians" *is* a better story.

BORGES:

But, perhaps, perhaps "The Form of the Sword" makes for easier reading?

BURGIN:

Yes, but what I'm saying is that essentially the person who was telling the story could have been either one of the men. Just like in "The Theologians," the two men were the same to God.

BORGES: Yes, that's true. I never thought of that.

BURGIN:

He could have been either one of the men and in a sense he was.

BORGES:

I never thought of that. Well, you have enriched the story. Thank you.

BURGIN:

You noticed something very interesting about Don Quixote. That he never does kill a man in all his adventures, although he often engages in fights.

BORGES: Ah yes! I wonder about that.

BURGIN: And then you wrote that parable.

BORGES:

Well, I suppose the real reason or the obvious reason would be that Cervantes wanted to keep within the limits of farce and had he killed a man, then the book, then that would have been too real, no? Don't you think so? I mean if Quixote kills a man, then he somehow is a real, bad man, whether he feels himself justified or not. I don't think Cervantes wanted to go as far as all that, no? He wanted to keep his book within certain bounds, and had Don Quixote killed a man that would have done Cervantes no good.

BURGIN:

Also, there's the idea you've mentioned that the author at some time in the book becomes the main character. So perhaps Cervantes couldn't bear to kill a man *himself,* if he *became* Don Quixote.

BORGES:

Yes, yet I suppose he must have killed many in his life, as

148

a soldier. But that's different, no? Because if a soldier kills a man, he kills him impersonally, no? Don't you think so? I mean if you kill a man as a soldier you don't really kill him. You're merely a tool. Or somebody else kills him through you or, well, you don't have to accept any responsibility. I don't think a soldier feels guilty about the people he's killed, no? Except the men who threw the bomb on Hiroshima.

BURGIN:

Well, some of them have gone insane, some of those people who were involved with the bomb.

BORGES:

Yes, but somehow, now I suppose you are, I shouldn't say this to you, I'll be blurting it out.

BURGIN: Well, say it.

BORGES:

I can't think of Hiroshima as being worse than any battle.

BURGIN: What do you mean?

BORGES:

It ended the war in a day. And the fact that many people are killed is the same fact that one man is killed. Because every man dies his own death and he would have died it anyhow. Then, well, of course, one hardly knows all the people who were killed in Hiroshima. After all, Japan was in favour of violence, of empire, of fighting, of being very cruel; they were not early Christians or anything of the kind. In fact, had they had the bomb, they would have done the same thing to America.

Hold it, I know that I shouldn't be saying these things because they make me seem very callous. But somehow I have never been able to feel that way about Hiroshima. Perhaps something new is happening to mankind, but I think that if you accept war, well, I should say this, if you accept war, you have to accept cruelty. And you have to accept slaughter and bloodshed and that kind of thing. And after all, to be killed by a rifle, or to be killed by a stone thrown at you, or by somebody thrusting a knife into you, is essentially the same. Hiroshima stands out, because many innocent people were involved and because the whole thing was packed into a single moment. But you know, after all, I don't see the difference between being in Hiroshima and a battle or, maybe I'm saying this for the sake of argument, or between Hiroshima and human life. I mean in Hiroshima the whole tragedy, the whole horror, is packed very close and you can see it very vividly. But the mere fact of man growing, and falling sick, and dying is Hiroshima spread out.

You understand what I mean? For example, there's a part in Cervantes and in Quevedo where they speak against firearms, no? Because they say that, after all, a man may be a good marksman and another may not be. No, but what I think is this: I think that really all arms are horrible, no? Are awful. We've grown more or less accustomed, our sensibilities have been blunted, by ages and ages and so we accept a sword. Or we accept a bayonet or a spear, and we accept firearms, but whenever a new arm is about, it seems peculiarly atrocious, though after all, if you are going to be killed, it hardly matters to you whether you are killed by a bomb, or by being knocked on the head, or by being knifed.

Of course, it might be said that war is essentially awful or rather that killing is essentially awful or perhaps that dying is essentially awful. But we have our sensibilities blunted, and when a new weapon appears, we think of it as being especially devilish—you remember that Milton makes the Devil invent gunpowder and artillery, no? Because in

150

those days artillery was sufficiently new to be specially awful. And perhaps a day will come when people will accept the atomic bomb when we shrink from some keener invention.

BURGIN:

Then it's a certain idea that you find awful. The idea of a man being killed.

BORGES:

Yes, but if you accept that, and all war accepts that, or else there would be no war ... even the idea of a man fighting a duel is the same idea essentially.

BURGIN:

Well, the soldier may accept it while he's fighting under orders, but I, as an individual, don't have to accept it. And the soldier may not be a person who thinks in terms of accepting something or not, he may just do something because he's told to by his government. He doesn't necessarily question it. Do you think that each soldier debates with himself whether a given war is right or not, or examines the reasons and debates whether it's worth taking another human life?

BORGES:

I don't think he has to. I don't think he could do it, no? Yet, I remember, my great-grandfather, Colonel Suárez, who had fought the War of Independence, the War of Brazil and the Civil War. When he was about to marry, his wife asked him about the men he had killed. And then he told her that he had only killed one man, and that was a Spaniard he had to run through with a lance in order to save a friend of his who had been taken prisoner. He said that was the one man he killed in the War of Independence, the War of Brazil and the Civil War. Now I suspect that he

151

was lying, but that he knew at the same time that she must have felt a kind of horror at the idea that she was going to give herself to a bloodstained man, no? So I suppose he invented that in order to calm her.

You remember, the battle of Junín lasted three quarters of an hour—not a shot was fired, the whole thing was done with spears and swords. It stands to reason that someone was going to get killed, and that he would have known it. And besides, I knew he had many executed. But I suppose that in a sense he felt that what he had done was awful, or rather, perhaps he felt that those things were awful to a woman but not to a man, no? I don't think he was a clear thinker or anything of the kind, but he must have felt what all soldiers feel, well, these things have to be done and I've done them, and I'm not ashamed of it, but why speak of those things to a woman who cannot be expected to understand. I suppose he was lying, because battles, well, they were very primitive in those days and quite small affairs, but the fact that they were primitive and small affairs may, I suppose—if a man killed anybody he had to be quite sure about it, no? Because if you are hacking away with a sword at somebody, you know whether you've killed him or not.

BURGIN:

I've always felt that by working out the rational consequences of mystic ideas, you've written about the things people are most astonished at or afraid of, that you've selected things to write about that are really even more terrifying than death, like infinity.

BORGES:

But I don't think of death as being terrifying. I was going over a sonnet with di Giovanni and the subject of that sonnet, I began by saying to the reader that he was invulnerable, that nothing could happen to him, that God had

152

given to him the certainty of dust, mortality, and that, after all, if one day he should die, he could always fall back on the fact that life was a mere dream. But I don't think of death as being terrifying.

BURGIN: What about infinity?

BORGES:
Infinity, yes, because infinity is an intellectual problem. Death means you stop being, you cease from thinking, or feeling, or wondering, and at least you're lucky in that you don't have to worry. You might as well worry, as the Latin poet said, about the ages and ages that preceded you when you did not exist. You might as well worry about the endless past as the endless future uninhabited by you. . . . Infinity, yes, that's a problem, but death isn't a problem in that sense. There's no difficulty whatever in imagining that even as I go to sleep every night, I may have a long sleep at the end. I mean it's not an intellectual problem. I don't understand Unamuno, because Unamuno wrote that God, for him, was the provider of immortality, that he couldn't believe in a God who didn't believe in immortality. I don't see that. There might be a God who might not want me to go on living, or who might think that the universe does not need me. After all, it did not need me until 1899, when I was born. I was left out until it did.

BURGIN:
Perhaps a stronger argument against God might be the idea of random happenings. The fact that people can be born as freaks, physical freaks, or that, people can be born paralysed.

BORGES:
Oh yes, of course. In fact, there are many arguments against God, but there are only four arguments for His existence.

153

BURGIN: Four arguments? Which are they?

BORGES:
Well, one is called the ontological argument, it seems to be a mere trick. It runs thus. Can you imagine a perfect being, all powerful, all wise, and so on, and then you say yes, no?

BURGIN: Yes.

BORGES: Now, does that being exist or not?

BURGIN:
Well, then the answer is, if you imagine him, he exists.

BORGES: No, no. Then you would say no, I don't know.

BURGIN: You have to say no?

BORGES:
Or, I don't know. Then here the argument is clinched, in a very unconvincing way as I see it. You said that you could imagine a perfect being, a being all wise, all knowing, well, if that being does not exist, then it isn't perfect. Because how can a nonexistent being be perfect. So you have to add existence to it. It's not a very convincing argument, no? And then it was made still worse. It went, does God exist? I don't know. Does a man exist? Well, he seems to exist. Then you think that God, who is eternal, omnipotent, and so on, cannot achieve what a man has to start with? And God, who is so wise, cannot even attain to manhood? Well, of course, that's not an argument. In fact, if you say that God cannot succeed in existing, you are really supposing there is existence, no? Because if you don't exist you cannot succeed or fail at it.

154

BURGIN:

Do you think that a lot of philosophy has been wasted arguing about the existence of God, or can you still derive enjoyment from it?

BORGES:

I can derive great enjoyment from it, the enjoyment I get out of detective novels or science fiction. Enjoyment of the imagination. But I don't think anybody could take it too seriously. Of course, you may believe in God, I daresay there is a God, but I don't believe in Him because of those arguments. I should say that I believe in God in spite of theology. Theologians follow the rules of the game; you accept certain premises and you have to accept the conclusions.

BURGIN:

You once said that if a man is happy, he doesn't want to write or really do anything, he just wants to be.

BORGES:

Yes, because happiness is an end in itself. That's one of the advantages, or perhaps the only advantage, of unhappiness. That unhappiness *has* to be transmuted into something.

BURGIN:

So then, your own writing proceeds out of a sense of sorrow.

BORGES:

I think that all writing comes out of unhappiness. I suppose that when Mark Twain was writing about Mississippi and about the rafts, I suppose he was simply looking at his own past, no? He had a kind of homesickness for the Mississippi. . . . Of course, when you're happy you don't need anything, no? Now I can be happy, but not for a long time.

BURGIN:

Walt Whitman tried to write some poems about happiness, but we see through them so that . . .

BORGES:

But Whitman, I think, overdid it. Because in him everything is wonderful, you know? I don't think that anybody could really believe that everything is wonderful, no? Except in a sense of it being a wonder. Of course, you can do without that particular kind of miracle. No, in the case of Whitman I think he thought it was his duty as an American to be happy. And that he had to cheer up his readers. Of course, he wanted to be unlike any other poet, but Whitman worked with a programme, I should say, he began with a theory and then he went on to his work. I don't think of him as a spontaneous writer.

BURGIN:

Although he tries to convey the impression of spontaneity.

BORGES: Well, he had to do it.

BURGIN: Do you think any poets are really spontaneous?

BORGES:

No, but I think that if you're writing about unhappiness, feeling bleak or discouraged, it can be done more sincerely. . . . Somebody wrote, I think it was William Henry Hudson, that he had tried to—I think he was quoting someone else— that he wanted to study philosophy and that he tried to read, well, I don't know, Hume or Spinoza, but he couldn't do it because happiness was always breaking in. He really was just bragging, no? In the case of most people, happiness isn't always breaking in, but if it breaks in, you are thankful for it.

156

BURGIN:

But don't you think many people are ashamed to admit they're happy? In fact, Bertrand Russell wrote a book called *The Right To Be Happy.*

BORGES:

Well, because people felt that if other people were unhappy, their happiness would be resented. I don't think we need be afraid of feeling too happy, no? For example, if suddenly, walking down the street or sitting here in my room, I feel happy, I think I'd better accept it and not pry into it. Because if I pry into it, I shall find that I have far to many reasons for being unhappy. But I think that one should accept happiness, and perhaps unexplained happiness is all to the better because I think that's something right in your body, no? Or in your mind. But if you're happy because of something that has happened, then you may be unhappy the next moment. I mean if you are just being spontaneously, innocently, happy, that's all to the good. Of course, that doesn't happen too often.

BURGIN:

You once said to me that you could envision a world without novels, but not without tales or verses. How do you feel about philosophy? Could you envision a world without philosophy?

BORGES:

No. I think that people who have no philosophy live a poor kind of life, no? People who are too sure about reality and about themselves. I think that philosophy helps you to live. For example, if you think of life as a dream, there may be something gruesome or uncanny about it, and you may sometimes feel that you are living in a nightmare, but if you think of reality as something hard and fast, that's still worse, no? I think that philosophy may give the world a kind of haziness, but that haziness is all to the good. If you're a materialist, if you believe in hard and fast things, then you're tied down by reality, or by what you call reality. So that, in a sense, philosophy dissolves reality, but as reality is not always too pleasant, you will be helped by that dissolution. Well, those are very obvious thoughts, of course, though they are none the less true for being obvious.

EPILOGUE

Through the years, a man peoples a space with images
of provinces, kingdoms, mountains, bays, ships,
islands, fishes, rooms, tools, stars, horses, and people.
Shortly before his death he discovers that the patient
labyrinth of lines traces the image of his own face.

—Jorge Luis Borges